1st EDITION

Perspectives on Diseases and Disorders

Cerebral Palsy

Jacqueline Langwith
Book Editor

Detroit • New York • San Francisco • New Haven, Conn • Waterville, Maine • London

Christine Nasso, *Publisher*
Elizabeth Des Chenes, *Managing Editor*

© 2011 Greenhaven Press, a part of Gale, Cengage Learning

For more information, contact:
Greenhaven Press
27500 Drake Rd.
Farmington Hills, MI 48331-3535
Or you can visit our Internet site at gale.cengage.com

Articles in Greenhaven Press anthologies are often edited for length to meet page requirements. In addition, original titles of these works are changed to clearly present the main thesis and to explicitly indicate the author's opinion. Every effort is made to ensure that Greenhaven Press accurately reflects the original intent of the authors. Every effort has been made to trace the owners of copyrighted material.

LIBRARY OF CONGRESS CATALOGING-IN-PUBLICATION DATA

Cerebral palsy / Jacqueline Langwith, book editor.
　 p. cm. -- (Perspectives on diseases and disorders)
　Includes bibliographical references and index.
　ISBN 978-0-7377-4998-4 (hardcover)
　1. Cerebral palsy--Popular works. I. Langwith, Jacqueline.
　RC388.C475 2011
　616.8'36--dc22
　　　　　　　　　　　　　　　　　　　　　　　　　　　　2010026765

Printed in the United States of America
1 2 3 4 5 6 7 14 13 12 11 10

CONTENTS

FOREWORD

"Medicine, to produce health, has to examine disease."
—Plutarch

Independent research on a health issue is often the first step to complement discussions with a physician. But locating accurate, well-organized, understandable medical information can be a challenge. A simple Internet search on terms such as "cancer" or "diabetes," for example, returns an intimidating number of results. Sifting through the results can be daunting, particularly when some of the information is inconsistent or even contradictory. The Greenhaven Press series Perspectives on Diseases and Disorders offers a solution to the often overwhelming nature of researching diseases and disorders.

From the clinical to the personal, titles in the Perspectives on Diseases and Disorders series provide students and other researchers with authoritative, accessible information in unique anthologies that include basic information about the disease or disorder, controversial aspects of diagnosis and treatment, and first-person accounts of those impacted by the disease. The result is a well-rounded combination of primary and secondary sources that, together, provide the reader with a better understanding of the disease or disorder.

Each volume in Perspectives on Diseases and Disorders explores a particular disease or disorder in detail. Material for each volume is carefully selected from a wide range of sources, including encyclopedias, journals, newspapers, nonfiction books, speeches, government documents, pamphlets, organization newsletters, and position papers. Articles in the first chapter provide an authoritative, up-to-date overview that covers symptoms, causes and effects, treatments, cures, and medical advances. The second chapter presents a substantial number of opposing viewpoints on controversial treatments and other current debates relating to the volume topic. The third chapter offers a variety of personal perspectives on the disease or disorder. Patients, doctors, caregivers, and loved ones represent just some of the voices found in this narrative chapter.

Each Perspectives on Diseases and Disorders volume also includes:

- An **annotated table of contents** that provides a brief summary of each article in the volume.
- An **introduction** specific to the volume topic.
- Full-color **charts and graphs** to illustrate key points, concepts, and theories.
- Full-color **photos** that show aspects of the disease or disorder and enhance textual material.
- **"Fast Facts"** that highlight pertinent additional statistics and surprising points.
- A **glossary** providing users with definitions of important terms.
- A **chronology** of important dates relating to the disease or disorder.
- An annotated list of **organizations to contact** for students and other readers seeking additional information.
- A **bibliography** of additional books and periodicals for further research.
- A detailed **subject index** that allows readers to quickly find the information they need.

Whether a student researching a disorder, a patient recently diagnosed with a disease, or an individual who simply wants to learn more about a particular disease or disorder, a reader who turns to Perspectives on Diseases and Disorders will find a wealth of information in each volume that offers not only basic information, but also vigorous debate from multiple perspectives.

INTRODUCTION

In the 2009 movie *Avatar*, Jake Sully, a paraplegic war veteran, "neurally" controls a nine-foot-tall avatar that lives with the Na'vi people on the planet Pandora. The first time Sully is connected to his avatar he runs as fast and as far as he can—something Sully can no longer do in his own body. Sully's joy is obvious as his avatar sinks its toes into the grass on Pandora. Many people who have cerebral palsy are, like Sully, using avatars to shed their wheelchairs and run as far and as fast as they can. The only difference between them and Sully is that their avatars do not live on the planet Pandora. They live in a virtual world created on the Internet called Second Life (SL). In Second Life, disabilities can remain hidden as people can create—and be—any kind of avatar they want. Many disabled persons create avatars that can walk; however, not all disabled people leave their wheelchairs behind when they become residents of Second Life.

Second Life is a colorful, picturesque, and often exotic world that exists in cyberspace. Anyone with a computer and an Internet connection can become an SL resident by going to www.secondlife.com and creating an avatar to inhabit and interact in SL's virtual world. Avatars can run, walk, and even fly around as they explore the many destinations available in SL. Avatars can visit places like Tuli Bahari, a surfing community, or Eloni, a snowy island. SL residents can meet other residents and listen to music at clubs like the Junkyard Blues, Jade's Jazz Lounge, or Blackhorse Country. In the *Second Life Quick Start Guide*, potential new residents are told, "In Second Life, there's always someone to talk to, dance with, learn from or perhaps even love. You can meet people all over the world without ever leaving your home. And here, there's no jet lag and the clubs are always open."

Second Life is appealing to many disabled persons because it provides them the experience of shedding their disability. In his book, *Coming of Age in Second Life: An Anthropologist Explores the Virtually Human*, Tom Boellstorff says that "some persons spend time in virtual worlds to be something different: women becoming men or men becoming women, adults becoming children, disabled persons walking, humans become animals, and so on." The experiences of Janna and Neils, two disabled persons quoted in an April 27, 2007, British Broadcasting Corporation story by Paul Crichton, illustrates Boellstorff's theory. Janna and Neils are confined to wheelchairs, but on SL their avatars walk, run, and fly. Janna says, "I have a disability. It sometimes makes it hard to get out of the house and meet people. In the virtual world I am not disabled. I am the girl who is able to run and play, like everyone else." Similarly, Neils says, "Literally being able to walk is a very strange experience for someone using a wheelchair in real life for more than 20 years now." Boellstorff notes that SL enables people to change any aspect of their avatar at will and thus to be whomever they want to be. As one SL resident quoted in Boellstorff's book says, being in SL means "you can be who you are, not [just] your body."

Not every disabled person on SL seeks to escape from his or her wheelchair, however. Simon Walsh is a thirty-something gay man from the UK who suffers from cerebral palsy. He was the first person to create an avatar with a wheelchair in the SL world. He also created a nightclub for his avatar and other disabled avatars to hang out at. Walsh's nightclub on SL is called "Wheelies," and it is particularly welcoming to people who use wheelchairs and other impairment-specific devices. For an article in the January 2010 issue of the University of Missouri journal, *Artifacts*, author Jamela Barry asked Simon

Walsh why his SL avatar uses a wheelchair. According to Barry, "Walsh's original reason for showing his disability within the virtual world was to save time from informing people of what he calls his 'cultural background' as a disabled person." Barry says Walsh appreciates his avatar as a symbolic representation of himself. "Having a virtual disability is about representing who I am," said Walsh. When asked why some disabled people choose able-bodied avatars and decide not to display their disability on SL, Walsh tells Barry, "Most people who choose not to display their disability on Second Life see their impairment as separate from their inner identity."

Some disabled people switch between able-bodied avatars and avatars that reveal their disability. Judith, a severely disabled woman with cerebral palsy from Sydney, Australia, is one of Walsh's friends on SL and a frequent visitor to Wheelies. Judith is in a wheelchair and operates her computer by way of a "headstick," which is a pointer

A disabled student at Keio University in Japan wears electrodes on his scalp to control his online character, or avatar, in the Second Life virtual reality world. **(Yuriko Nakao/ Reuters/Landov)**

attached to her forehead with straps around her head and chin. In 2007, Judith was interviewed by Roger Hudson, a computer accessibility expert, about her experiences as a disabled person on SL. Judith's avatar has a wheelchair in SL, but she doesn't always stay in it. When asked about this, Judith tells Roger, "Just like in real life, I find the attitude of people in Second Life to people with disabilities [to be disappointing]. I have run an experiment myself. I've gone to this particular website as an able bodied person, got out on the dance floor and danced for half an hour with different avatars or different people, or whatever you call them. Then I've gone away, put myself in my wheelchair, gone back, [and] the same people were there, and they didn't want to know me." Virtual worlds may appear to be fantasy spaces sealed off from the real world, but, as Judith's experience shows, real world attitudes—such as discrimination or indifference to the disabled—often cross the border between the two worlds.

Many adults with cerebral palsy who are confined to wheelchairs or use assistive walking devices are inhabiting virtual worlds like Second Life. For some of them, like Janna and Neils, Second Life can be a place to escape from their disabilities. For others, like Simon and Judith, it is a place to affirm who they are, including that they are disabled. In *Perspectives on Diseases and Disorders: Cerebral Palsy*, the authors explain that some researchers are trying to understand and prevent the occurrence of cerebral palsy, while others are trying to develop ways to make life easier for those who struggle with the effects of the disorder. Contributors also debate many of the controversial issues surrounding cerebral palsy. Finally, the book presents the voices of individuals who live with cerebral palsy.

CHAPTER 1

Understanding Cerebral Palsy

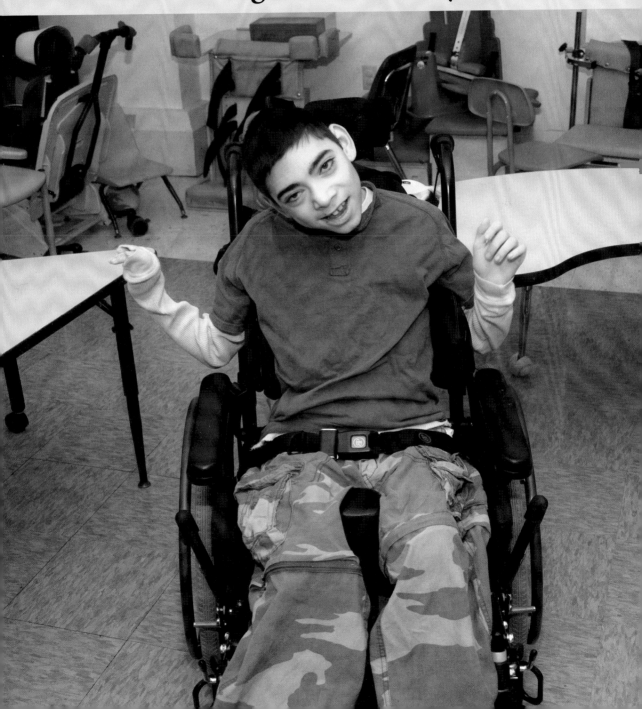

An Overview of Cerebral Palsy

Scott J. Polzin, Teresa G. Odle, and Tish Davidson

In the following article, Scott J. Polzin, Teresa G. Odle, and Tish Davidson provide an overview of cerebral palsy. According to the authors, cerebral palsy is a group of nonprogressive neurological and physical problems that occur as a result of brain damage either before, during, or shortly after birth. In people with cerebral palsy the brain sends out defective messages to various muscles causing them to involuntarily tighten, relax, or move uncontrollably. Cerebral palsy cannot be cured. The authors describe several treatments, however, that help to lessen the symptoms; these include medications, physical or occupational therapy, and surgery. Polzin, Odle, and Davidson are nationally published medical writers.

Photo on previous page. Cerebral palsy is a group of disorders of movement and posture caused by damage to the motor-control centers of the brain. (Ellen B. Senisi/Photo Researchers, Inc.)

Cerebral palsy (CP) is the term used for a group of nonprogressive disorders of movement and posture caused by damage to motor control centers of the brain either before, during, or after birth up to age two. The abnormalities of muscle control that define CP are often accompanied by other neurological and physical abnormalities.

CP is not a specific disorder but describes a broad group of neurological and physical problems. It encompasses disorders that arise from abnormal functioning of the cerebral cortex, a part of the brain that controls voluntary muscle movement. Damage to the brain occurs any time between conception and age two. CP is not progressive, meaning that it does not get worse with time. In fact, with treatment, many children improve. CP is also called static (not worsening) encephalopathy (a disease of the brain). CP is a movement disorder of the brain only. It does not include disorders of muscle control that arise in the muscles themselves or disorders in the peripheral nervous system (nerves outside the brain and spinal cord).

The symptoms of CP and their severity are variable. Those with mild CP may have only minor difficulty with fine motor skills, such as grasping and manipulating items with their hands. Severe CP can involve significant muscle problems in all four limbs, mental retardation, seizures, and difficulties with vision, speech, and hearing.

In individuals with CP, the muscles that receive defective messages from the brain may be constantly contracted and tight (spastic), excessively loose (hypotonic), exhibit involuntary writhing movements (athetosis), or resist or make uncontrolled voluntary movement (dyskinesia). Balance and coordination may also be affected (ataxia). A combination of any of these problems, along with impairment in vision, hearing, and cognition (mental abilities) may also occur.

Forms of Cerebral Palsy

There are several forms of CP. Between 70% and 80% of individuals with CP have spastic CP. With spastic CP, the muscles are stiff and movements are difficult. Any or all

Lobes of the Cerebral Cortex

Cerebral palsy arises from abnormal functioning of the cerebral cortex, which is the heavily folded outer layer of the brain. It is divided into two hemispheres, each of which contains four lobes. The cerebral cortex directs the brain's higher cognitive and emotional functions.

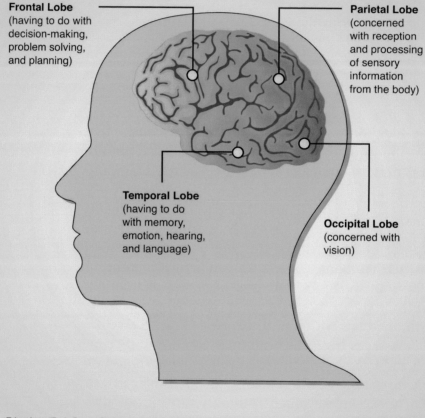

Frontal Lobe
(having to do with decision-making, problem solving, and planning)

Parietal Lobe
(concerned with reception and processing of sensory information from the body)

Temporal Lobe
(having to do with memory, emotion, hearing, and language)

Occipital Lobe
(concerned with vision)

Taken from: "Brain Power! Challenge: Grades 6–9," Module 1: An Introduction to the Brain and Nervous System, September 19, 2009. www.drugabuse.gov/JSP4/Mo001/page3.htm.

of the four limbs and trunk may be affected. When muscles are affected in only one limb, the condition is called monoplegia. When both arms or both legs are affected, it is called diplegia. Symptoms in both limbs on one side of the body is called hemiplegia, and when all four limbs

PERSPECTIVES ON DISEASES AND DISORDERS

are affected, the condition is called quadriplegia. Muscles of the trunk, neck, and head may be affected as well as the limbs. The most severe cases are often accompanied by difficulty with the muscles of the tongue and mouth, problems speaking, and mental retardation.

About 10% of people with CP have athetoid or dyskinetic cerebral palsy. This form of the disorder affects the entire body, with some muscles tight and spastic and others excessively loose. The lack of uniform muscle tone makes it difficult to control voluntary movements, and many coordinated activities such as walking are difficult or impossible.

Another 5–10% of individuals with CP have a form known as ataxic cerebral palsy. Ataxic CP affects the whole body and interferes with balance and coordination. People with this form of CP may have difficulty walking or coordinating activities such as getting food from plate to mouth with an eating utensil.

The rate of CP in the United States is the same as in other countries worldwide and is between 1.5 and 2 children per 1,000 births. In 2007, about half a million people in the United States were living with CP and about 6,000 new cases were being diagnosed annually. CP affects all races equally, although some studies suggest that low socioeconomic status may increase the risk of having a child with CP.

CP is caused by damage to the brain any time before birth, during the birthing process, or up to age two. For many years, it was believed that most cases of CP were due to brain injuries occurring during a traumatic birth from lack of oxygen (asphyxia). However, recent research has shown that fewer than 10% of CP [cases] can be attributed to asphyxia during a difficult delivery. Research also suggests that although some hereditary/genetic syndromes have signs and symptoms that mimic CP, CP is not inherited.

Prenatal Causes

About 70% of cases of CP can be traced to an event that happens before birth. The complicated process of fetal brain development is susceptible to many chance errors that can result in abnormalities of varying degree. Some of these errors result in structural or functional abnormalities of the brain. The fetal brain is also vulnerable when exposed to maternal diseases and toxic substances.

Prematurity is a risk factor for CP. Advances in the medical care of premature infants have dramatically increased the rate of survival of these fragile newborns. However, as gestational age at delivery and birth weight of a baby decrease, the risk for CP dramatically increases. Infants born weighing less than 3.3 lb (1.5 kg) have a 30 times greater chance of having CP than full-term babies.

Two factors are involved in the risk for CP associated with prematurity. First, premature babies are at higher risk for various CP-associated medical complications, such as intracerebral hemorrhage (bleeding in the brain), infection, and difficulty in breathing. Second, the onset of premature labor may be induced, in part, by complications that have already caused neurologic damage in the fetus. A combination of both factors almost certainly plays a role in some cases of CP.

The increase in multiple pregnancies that has resulted from an increased use of fertility drugs has increased the risks for developmental abnormalities and premature delivery. Children from twin pregnancies have four times the risk of developing CP as children from singleton pregnancies, owing to the fact that more twin pregnancies are delivered prematurely. The risk for CP in a triplet birth is up to 18 times greater than that of a singleton pregnancy.

Several maternal-fetal infections are known to increase the risk for CP, including rubella (German measles), cytomegalovirus (CMV), and toxoplasmosis. Each of these infections is a risk to the fetus only if the mother contracts it for the first time during pregnancy. Even then, most exposed babies will not develop CP. Most women are immune to all three infections by the time they reach childbearing age. A woman's immune status can be determined using the so-called TORCH (for Toxoplasmosis, Rubella, Cytomegalovirus, and Herpes) test before or during pregnancy.

Researchers have also linked prenatal CP to an infection of the placental membranes (chorioamnionitis). This infection increases the risk of CP in both premature and full-term infants. Maternal infections of the reproductive system and urinary tract during pregnancy may also increase the risk of the infant developing CP.

Other potential prenatal events that may increase the risk of CP include any action that results in insufficient oxygen reaching the fetus, such as serious physical trauma to the mother's uterus during pregnancy. Other risk factors are maternal exposure to toxins (poisons) such as mercury, certain blood disorders, and abnormal maternal thyroid function.

> **FAST FACT**
>
> Each year twelve hundred to fifteen hundred preschool-age children are recognized as having cerebral palsy, according to the United Cerebral Palsy organization.

Perinatal Causes

The perinatal period is the time around which the birth takes place. About 10% of CP arises from events in the perinatal period. Birth asphyxia occurs when the fetus fails to get enough oxygen during labor and delivery. Birth asphyxia significant enough to result in CP, although relatively rare in developed countries, is a leading cause of perinatal CP. Tight nuchal cord (umbilical cord around the infant's neck) and prolapsed cord (umbilical cord delivered before the baby) may cause birth asphyxia, as may heavy bleeding and other complications associated with placental abruption and placenta previa (placenta lying over the cervix).

Incompatibility between the Rh blood types of mother and child (mother Rh negative, fetus Rh positive) can result in severe anemia in the baby (erythroblastosis fetalis).

This may lead to other complications, including severe jaundice, which can cause CP. Rh incompatibility disease in the newborns is now rare in developed countries due to routine screening of maternal blood type and prenatal treatment of at risk pregnancies. The routine, effective treatment of jaundice due to other causes has also made it an infrequent cause of CP in developed countries.

Postnatal Causes

The remaining 15% of CP arises from neurologic injury sustained after birth and before age two. CP that has a postnatal cause is sometimes referred to as acquired CP, but this is only accurate for those cases caused by infection or trauma.

Serious infections that affect the brain directly, such as meningitis and encephalitis, may cause irreversible damage to the brain and result in CP. Birth defects that become apparent only in early childhood may also cause CP or CP-like symptoms.

Physical trauma to an infant or child resulting in brain injury, such as physical abuse, accidents, near drowning, or suffocation, can cause CP. Likewise, ingestion of a toxic substance such as lead, mercury, poisons, or certain chemicals can cause neurological damage, as can accidental overdose of certain medications.

Symptoms Often Change

By definition, the defect in cerebral function causing CP is nonprogressive. Nevertheless, the symptoms of CP often change over time. Most symptoms of CP relate in some way to the abnormal control of muscles. CP is categorized first by the type of movement/postural disturbance(s) present, then by a description of which limbs are affected, and finally by the severity of motor impairment. For example, spastic diplegia refers to continuously tight muscles where there is no voluntary control in both legs, while athetoid quadraparesis describes uncontrolled writhing movements and muscle weakness in all four limbs. These three-part descriptions are helpful in providing a general picture, but cannot give a complete description of an individual with CP. CP can also be loosely categorized as mild, moderate, or severe. Mild CP or severe CP refers not only to the number of symptoms present, but also to the level of involvement of any particular class of symptoms. Nevertheless, these are very subjective terms with no firm boundaries between them.

A muscle that is tensed and contracted is called hypertonic, while excessively loose muscles are hypotonic. Spastic hypertonic muscles can cause serious orthopedic problems, including scoliosis (spine curvature), hip dislocation, or contractures. A contracture is a shortening of a muscle, aided sometimes by a weak-opposing force from a neighboring muscle. Contractures may become permanent, or "fixed," without therapeutic intervention.

Fixed contractures may cause postural abnormalities in the affected limbs. Clenched fists and contracted feet (equinus or equinovarus) are common in people with CP. Spasticity in the thighs causes them to turn in and cross at the knees, resulting in an unusual method of walking known as a "scissors gait." Any of the joints in the limbs may be stiff and difficult to move due to spasticity of the attached muscles. Athetosis (writhing movements) and dyskinesia (uncontrolled movements) often occur in combination with spasticity, but do not often occur alone. The same is true of ataxia (impaired coordination of movements).

Mechanisms that cause CP are not always restricted to motor-control areas of the brain. Other neurologically based symptoms may include:

- mental retardation/learning disabilities
- behavioral disorders
- seizure disorders
- visual impairment
- hearing loss
- speech impairment (dysarthria)
- abnormal sensation and perception

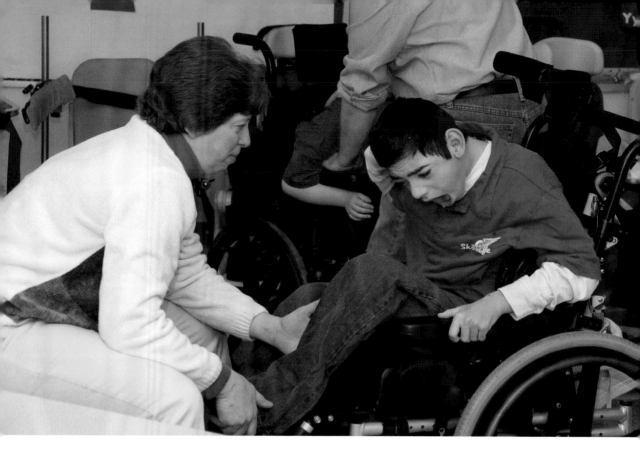

Severe cerebral palsy can involve muscle problems in all four limbs, mental retardation, seizures, and difficulties in speech, vision, and hearing. (Ellen B. Senisi/ Photo Researchers, Inc.)

These problems may have as great or greater an impact on a child's life as the physical impairments of CP, although not all children with CP are affected by other problems. Many infants and children with CP have growth impairment. About one-third of individuals with CP have moderate-to-severe mental retardation, one-third have mild mental retardation, and one-third have normal intelligence.

Diagnosis

No single test is diagnostic for CP, but certain factors increase suspicion of the disorder. The Apgar score measures an infant's condition immediately after birth on a scale from one to ten. Infants with low Apgar scores are at increased risk for CP. Presence of abnormal muscle tone or movements may indicate CP, as may the persistence of infantile reflexes. Imaging of the brain using ultrasound, X-rays, MRI [magnetic resonance imaging], and/or CT [computed tomography] scans may reveal a structural anomaly. Some brain lesions associated with CP include scarring, cysts, expansion of the cerebral ventricles (hydrocephalus), periventricular leukomalacia (an abnormality of the area surrounding the ventricles), areas of dead tissue (necrosis), and evidence of an intracerebral hemorrhage or blood clot. Blood and urine biochemical tests, as well as genetic tests, may be used to rule out other possible causes, including muscle and peripheral nerve diseases, mitochondrial and metabolic diseases, and other inherited disorders. Evaluations by a pediatric developmental specialist and a geneticist may be of benefit.

The signs of CP are not usually noticeable at birth. Healthy children progress through a predictable set of developmental milestones through the first 18 months of life. Children with CP, however, tend to reach these milestones more slowly because of their motor impairments. Delays in reaching common developmental milestones are usually the first symptoms of CP. Infants with more severe cases of CP are usually diagnosed earlier than others with mild cases.

Selected developmental milestones and the ages for normally acquiring them are given below. If a child does not acquire the skill by the age shown in parentheses, there is some cause for concern, and a pediatrician should be consulted for additional evaluation.

- sits well unsupported—6 months (8–10 months)
- babbles—6 months (8 months)
- crawls—9 months (12 months)
- finger feeds, holds bottle—9 months (12 months)
- walks alone—12 months (15–18 months)
- uses one or two words other than dada/mama—12 months (15 months)
- walks up and down steps—24 months (24–36 months)
- turns pages in books; removes shoes and socks—24 months (30 months)

Children do not normally favor one hand consistently over the other before 12–18 months of age. Strong hand preference before this age may be a sign that the child has difficulty using the other hand. This same preference for one side of the body may show up as asymmetric crawling or favoring one leg while climbing stairs.

Normal, healthy children progress at somewhat different rates, and slow beginning accomplishment is often followed by normal development. Other causes for developmental delay—some benign, some serious—should be excluded before considering CP. CP is nonprogressive, so loss of previously acquired skills indicates that CP is not the cause of the problem.

Treatment and Prognosis

Cerebral palsy cannot be cured, but many of the disabilities it causes can be managed through planning and timely care. Treatment for a child with CP depends on the severity, nature, and location of the primary muscular symptoms, as well as any associated problems that might be present. Optimal care of a child with mild CP may involve regular interaction with only a physical therapist and occupational therapist, whereas care for a more severely affected child may include visits to multiple medical specialists throughout life.

Spasticity, muscle weakness, poor coordination, ataxia, and scoliosis are all significant impairments that affect the posture and mobility of a person with CP. Physical and occupational therapists work with the patient and the family to maximize the ability to move affected limbs, develop normal motor patterns, and maintain posture. Assistive technology—things such as wheelchairs, walkers, shoe inserts, crutches, and braces—are often required. A speech therapist and aids such as computer-controlled communication devices can make a tremendous difference in the life of those who have speech impairments.

Therapy must be highly individualized because of the variety of symptoms CP causes.

A variety of drugs are used to treat specific symptoms. The following types are the most commonly used:

- anticonvulsants such as valproic acid (Depakote, Depakene, Depacon) and phenobarbitol used to treat seizures
- muscle relaxants such as Baclofen (Lioresal) used to treat excessive contractions
- benzodiazepines such as diazepam (Valium) to treat seizures
- dopamine precursor drugs such as levodopa/carbidopa (Sinemet, Sinemet CR) used to treat tremors
- anticholinergics such as trihexyphenidyl (Artane, Trihexy) used to treat tremor and rigidity
- toxins such as botulinum toxin type A (Botox) used to treat abnormally strong contractions

Fixed contractures may be treated with either serial casting [wearing a succession of casts] or surgery. The most commonly used surgical procedures are tenotomy, tendon transfer, and dorsal rhizotomy. In tenotomy, tendons of the affected muscle are cut and the limb is cast in a more normal position while the tendon regrows. Alternatively, tendon transfer involves cutting and reattaching a tendon at a different point on the bone to enhance the length and function of the muscle. A neurosurgeon performing dorsal rhizotomy carefully cuts selected nerve roots in the spinal cord to prevent them from stimulating the spastic muscles. Neurosurgical techniques in the brain such as implanting tiny electrodes directly into the cerebellum, or cutting a portion of the hypothalamus, have very specific uses and have had mixed results.

Parents of a child newly diagnosed with CP are not likely to have the necessary expertise to coordinate the full range of care their child will need. Although knowledgeable and caring medical professionals are indispensable for developing a care plan, an important source of information and advice is other parents who have dealt with the same set of difficulties. Support groups for parents of children with CP can be significant sources of both practical advice and emotional support. Many cities have support groups that can be located through the United Cerebral Palsy Association, and most large medical centers have special multidisciplinary clinics for children with developmental disorders. . . .

Cerebral palsy can affect every stage of maturation, from childhood through adolescence to adulthood. At each stage, those with CP, along with their caregivers, must work to achieve the fullest range of experiences and education consistent with their abilities. The advice and intervention of various professionals remains crucial for people with CP. Although CP itself is not a terminal disorder, it can affect a person's lifespan by increasing the risk for certain medical problems. People with mild cerebral palsy may have near-normal lifespans, but the lifespan of those with more severe forms may be shortened. However, more than 90% of infants with CP survive into adulthood.

Cerebral Palsy Research Focuses on Prevention and Treatment

National Institute of Neurological Disorders and Stroke

In the following report the National Institute of Neurological Disorders and Stroke (NINDS) discusses the range of research being done on cerebral palsy. According to NINDS, researchers are trying to understand what happens early in fetal brain development that causes cerebral palsy. They are particularly interested in the process called "neuronal migration," where nerve cells travel to their appropriate places in the brain. The authors indicate that researchers are also interested in the role of brain chemicals and premature birth in the cause of cerebral palsy. The National Institute of Neurological Disorders and Stroke is one of twenty-seven institutes and centers of the National Institutes of Health. The mission of NINDS is to reduce the burden of neurological diseases in the United States.

Investigators from many fields of medicine and health are using their expertise to help improve the treatment and diagnosis of cerebral palsy. Much of their work is supported through the NINDS [National

SOURCE: The National Institute of Neurological Disorders and Stroke, "Cerebral Palsy: Hope Through Research," December 18, 2009.

Institute of Neurological Disorders and Stroke], the National Institute of Child Health and Human Development (NICHD), other agencies within the federal government, nonprofit groups such as the United Cerebral Palsy Research and Educational Foundation, and other private institutions.

The ultimate hope for curing cerebral palsy rests with prevention. In order to prevent cerebral palsy, however, scientists have to understand normal fetal brain development so that they can understand what happens when a baby's brain develops abnormally.

Understanding Abnormal Brain Development

Between conception and the birth of a baby, one cell divides to form a handful of cells, and then hundreds, millions, and, eventually, billions of cells. Some of these cells specialize to become brain cells, and then specialize even further into particular types of neurons that travel to their appropriate place in the brain (a process that scientists call *neuronal migration*). Once they are in the right place, they establish connections with other brain cells. This is how the brain develops and becomes able to communicate with the rest of the body—through overlapping neural circuits made up of billions of interconnected and interdependent neurons.

Many scientists now think that a significant number of children develop cerebral palsy because of mishaps early in brain development. They are examining how brain cells specialize and form the right connections, and they are looking for ways to prevent the factors that disrupt the normal processes of brain development.

Genetic defects are sometimes responsible for the brain malformations and abnormalities that cause cerebral palsy. Scientists funded by the NINDS are searching for the genes responsible for these abnormalities by collecting DNA samples from people with cerebral palsy and their families and using genetic screening techniques to discover linkages between individual genes and specific types of abnormality—primarily those associated with abnormal neuronal migration.

The Importance of Brain Chemicals

Scientists are scrutinizing events in newborn babies' brains, such as bleeding, epileptic seizures, and breathing and circulation problems, which can cause the abnormal release of chemicals that trigger the kind of damage that causes cerebral palsy. For example, research has shown that bleeding in the brain unleashes dangerously high amounts of a brain chemical called glutamate. Although glutamate is necessary in the brain to help neurons communicate, too much glutamate overexcites and kills neurons. Scientists are now looking closely at glutamate to detect how its release harms brain tissue. By learning how brain chemicals that are normally helpful become dangerously toxic, scientists will have opportunities to develop new drugs to block their harmful effects.

Scientists funded by the NINDS are also investigating whether substances in the brain that protect neurons from damage, called *neurotrophins*, could be used to prevent brain damage as a result of stroke or oxygen deprivation. Understanding how these *neuroprotective* substances act would allow scientists to develop synthetic neurotrophins that could be given immediately after injury to prevent neuron death and damage.

The relationship between uterine infections during pregnancy and the risk of cerebral palsy continues to be studied by researchers funded by the NIH [National Institutes of Health]. There is evidence that uterine infections trigger inflammation and the production of immune system cells called cytokines, which can pass into

FAST FACT

The prevalence rate of cerebral palsy among eight-year-old children is 3.1 per 1000, according to the most recent surveillance data from the Metropolitan Atlanta Developmental Disabilities Study.

an unborn baby's brain and interrupt normal development. By understanding what cytokines do in the fetal brain and the type of damage these immune system cells cause, researchers have the potential to develop medications that could be given to mothers with uterine infections to prevent brain damage in their unborn children.

The Risk of Premature Birth

Approximately 10 percent of newborns are born prematurely, and of those babies, more than 10 percent will have brain injuries that will lead to cerebral palsy and other brain-based disabilities. A particular type of damage to the white matter of the brain, called periventricular leukomalacia (PVL), is the predominant form of brain injury in premature infants. NINDS-sponsored researchers studying PVL are looking for new strategies to prevent this kind of damage by developing safe, nontoxic therapies delivered to at-risk mothers to protect their unborn babies.

Although congenital cerebral palsy is a condition that is present at birth, a year or two can pass before any disabilities are noticed. Researchers have shown that the earlier rehabilitative treatment begins, the better the outcome for children with cerebral palsy. But an early diagnosis is hampered by the lack of diagnostic techniques to identify brain damage or abnormalities in infants.

Research funded by the NINDS is using imaging techniques, devices that measure electrical activity in the brain, and neurobehavioral tests to predict those preterm infants who will develop cerebral palsy. If these screening techniques are successful, doctors will be able to identify infants at risk for cerebral palsy before they are born.

Noninvasive methods to record the brain activity of unborn babies in the womb and to identify those with brain damage or abnormalities would also be a valuable addition to the diagnostic tool kit. Another NINDS-funded study focuses on the development of fetal magnetoencephalography (fMEG)—a technology that would allow doctors to look for abnormalities in fetal brain activity.

Epidemiological studies—studies that look at the distribution and causes of disease among people—help scientists understand risk factors and outcomes for particular diseases and medical conditions. Researchers have

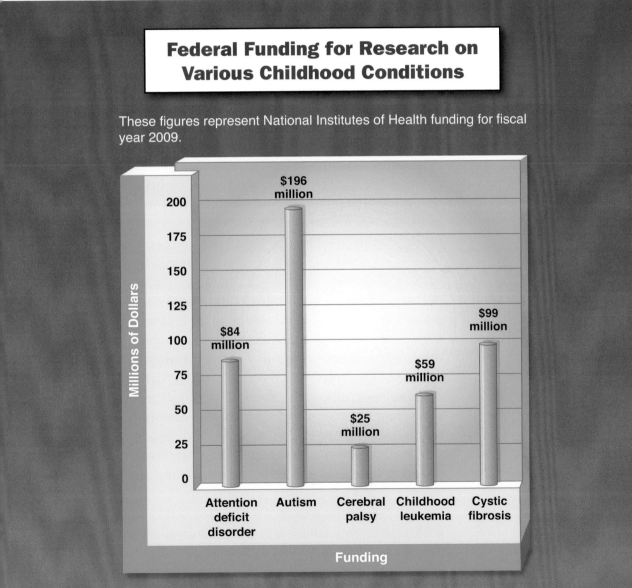

Federal Funding for Research on Various Childhood Conditions

These figures represent National Institutes of Health funding for fiscal year 2009.

Taken from: "Estimates of Funding for Various Research, Condition, and Disease Categories (RCDC)," National Institutes of Health, February 1, 2010. http://report.nih.gov/rcdc/categories/#bpopup.

established that preterm birth (when a baby is born before 32 weeks' gestation) is the highest risk factor for cerebral palsy. Consequently, the increasing rate of premature births in the United States puts more babies at risk. A large, long-term study funded by the NIH is following a group of more than 400 mothers and their infants born between 24 and 31 weeks' gestation. They are looking for relationships between preterm birth, maternal uterine infection, fetal exposure to infection, and short-term and long-term health and neurological outcomes. The researchers are hoping to discover environmental or lifestyle factors, or particular characteristics of mothers, which might protect preterm babies from neurological disabilities.

Evaluating Cerebral Palsy Treatments

While this research offers hope for preventing cerebral palsy in the future, ongoing research to improve treatment brightens the outlook for those who must face the challenges of cerebral palsy today. An important thrust of such research is the evaluation of treatments already in use so that physicians and parents have valid information to help them choose the best therapy. A good example of this effort is an ongoing NINDS-supported study that promises to yield new information about which patients are most likely to benefit from selective dorsal rhizotomy, a surgical technique that is increasingly being used to reduce spasticity.

Similarly, although physical therapy programs are used almost universally to rehabilitate children with cerebral palsy, there are no definitive studies to indicate which techniques work best. For example, constraint-induced therapy (CIT) is a type of physical therapy that has been used successfully with adult stroke survivors and individuals who have traumatic brain injury and are left with a weak or disabled arm on one side of the body. The therapy involves restraining the stronger arm in a cast and forcing the weaker arm to perform 6 hours of intensive

"shaping" activities every day over the course of 3 weeks. The researchers who conducted the clinical trials in adult stroke survivors realized CIT's potential for strengthening children's arms weakened by cerebral palsy.

In a randomized, controlled study of children with cerebral palsy funded by the NIH, researchers put one group of children through conventional physical therapy and another group through 21 consecutive days of CIT. Researchers looked for evidence of improvement in the movement and function of the disabled arm, whether the improvement lasted after the end of treatment, and if it was associated with significant gains in other areas, such as trunk control, mobility, communication, and self-help skills.

Children receiving CIT outperformed the children receiving conventional physical therapy across all measures of success, including how well they could move their arms after therapy and their ability to do new tasks during the study and then at home with their families. Six months later they still had better control of their arm.

A stroke victim practices constraint-induced therapy (CIT) which stimulates brain growth. Researchers think CIT has potential for strengthening children's muscles weakened by cerebral palsy. (**Bernard Troncale/Birmingham News/Landov**)

The results from this study are the first to prove the benefits of a physical therapy. Additional research to determine the optimal length and intensity of CIT will allow doctors to add this therapy to the cerebral palsy treatment toolbox.

Studies have shown that functional electrical stimulation is an effective way to target and strengthen spastic muscles, but the method of delivering the electrical pulses requires expensive, bulky devices implanted by a surgeon, or skin surface stimulation applied by a trained therapist. NINDS-funded researchers have developed a high-tech method that does away with the bulky apparatus and lead wires by using a hypodermic needle to inject microscopic wireless devices into specific muscles or nerves. The devices are powered by a telemetry wand that can direct the number and strength of their pulses by remote control. The device has been used to activate and strengthen muscles in the hand, shoulder, and ankle in people with cerebral palsy as well as in stroke survivors.

As researchers continue to explore new treatments for cerebral palsy and to expand our knowledge of brain development, we can expect significant improvements in the care of children with cerebral palsy and many other disorders that strike in early life.

New Chemicals May Help Prevent Cerebral Palsy

Megan Fellman

In the following article Megan Fellman discusses research findings of Northwestern University chemists that may lead to the prevention of cerebral palsy (CP). Fellman describes how the chemists collaborated with researchers at the NorthShore University HealthSystem and Chancellor University in Cleveland, Ohio, to find two powerful chemicals that show promise for preventing cerebral palsy. The chemicals prevent the production of nitric oxide in brain cells, which is thought to play a key role in causing congenital cerebral palsy (the type of CP present at birth). Fellman is the science and engineering editor for the news center at Northwestern University, a private research university in Evanston, Illinois.

Two [chemical] compounds developed by Northwestern University chemists have been shown to be effective in pre-clinical trials in protecting against cerebral palsy, a condition caused by neurodegeneration that affects body movement and muscle coordination.

SOURCE: Megan Fellman, "Stunning Finding: Compounds Protect Against Cerebral Palsy," Northwestern University Newscenter, February 24, 2009. Reproduced by permission.

"The results were just stunning, absolutely amazing," said Richard B. Silverman, John Evans Professor of Chemistry in the Weinberg College of Arts and Sciences at Northwestern, who led the drug development effort. "There was a remarkable difference between animals treated with a small dose of one of our compounds and those that were not."

The findings, which are published online by the journal *Annals of Neurology* [February 2009], suggest that a preventive strategy for cerebral palsy may be feasible for humans in the future. . . .

None of the fetuses born to animals treated with the two compounds died; more than half of those born to untreated animals died. Eighty-three percent of animals treated with one of the compounds were born normal, with no cerebral palsy characteristics. Sixty-nine percent of animals treated with the other compound were born normal. There was no sign of toxicity in the treated animals, and their blood pressure was normal.

Cerebral palsy is caused by an injury to the brain before, during or shortly after birth, although it typically is not diagnosed until after the age of one. Approximately 750,000 children and adults in the United States have a form of cerebral palsy, with the majority having been born with the condition.

Lowering Nitric Oxide Levels Is Key

The new compounds Silverman and his team developed inhibit an enzyme found in brain cells that produces nitric oxide, thus lowering nitric oxide levels. At normal levels, nitric oxide acts as a neurotransmitter [a chemical that carries messages between brain cells] and is important to neuronal [nerve cell] functioning, but at high levels it has been shown to damage brain tissue. An overabundance of nitric oxide is believed to play a role in cerebral palsy.

Two Chemicals Protect Baby Rabbits from Developing Neurological Symptoms

This graph shows the results of a trial in which baby rabbits were exposed to hypoxia-ischemia (inadequate blood and oxygen flow to the brain). Some were given a blank (saline) solution, while others were given either chemical "A" or chemical "B."

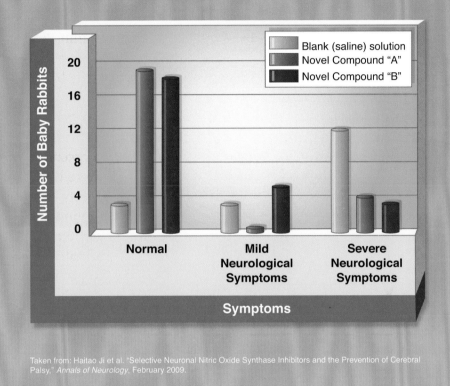

Taken from: Haitao Ji et al. "Selective Neuronal Nitric Oxide Synthase Inhibitors and the Prevention of Cerebral Palsy," *Annals of Neurology,* February 2009.

After a lengthy drug development process, Silverman went to his collaborator Sidhartha Tan, M.D., a neonatologist from NorthShore University HealthSystem [in Evanston, Illinois,] to test the two best compounds on Tan's cerebral palsy animal model. A diminished supply of oxygen (hypoxia) from mother to fetus causes an increase in nitric oxide levels in the brain, which leads to brain damage and newborns with cerebral palsy characteristics.

Silverman and Tan wanted to see if they could prevent brain damage in the fetuses by administering one of the compounds to the mother before the hypoxic event.

They expected some degree of success but were surprised by how effective the treatment was. The researchers attribute the protection from cerebral palsy to the decrease in the brain enzyme and the nitric oxide that is produced.

"We still have to bring the phenomenon to humans, which would be very exciting," said Tan, who has been investigating the impact of nitric oxide on neuronal damage. "There is such a dire need. If we could safely give the drug early to mothers in at-risk situations, we could prevent the fetal brain injury that results in cerebral palsy."

Drugs That Work Only in Brain Cells

In developing the potential drugs, Silverman and his team were able to produce something that pharmaceutical companies so far have not: highly selective compounds that inhibit the enzyme found in brain cells that produces nitric oxide but that do not affect similar nitric oxide–producing enzymes found in endothelial and macrophage cells.

Endothelial cells regulate blood pressure, and macrophage cells play an important role in the immune system. Reducing their production of nitric oxide would have deleterious effects on an animal, such as increasing blood pressure or compromising the immune system.

"The challenge was to lower only the nitric oxide in the brain and not in the other cells where the nitric oxide is very important," said Silverman, a member of Northwestern's Center for Drug Discovery and Chemical Biology.

"Early compounds developed by drug companies to target the brain enzyme actually bound to all three nitric

FAST FACT

According to the Centers for Disease Control and Prevention, about ten thousand babies born in the United States each year will develop cerebral palsy.

oxide enzymes," he said. "This made me think that the three enzymes must be very similar in structure. We decided to look for differences away from the normal binding site to get selectivity for only the brain enzyme."

The Collaborative Process

This approach paid off. Silverman and his team started with a molecule that showed good selectivity of the brain enzyme over the macrophage enzyme but with no selectivity over the endothelial enzyme. The researchers then made modifications to the molecule and built a library of 185 different compounds that could be tested for the selectivity they wanted. They found 10 good ones. More modifications were made until they had a few compounds that were very selective and very potent for the brain enzyme.

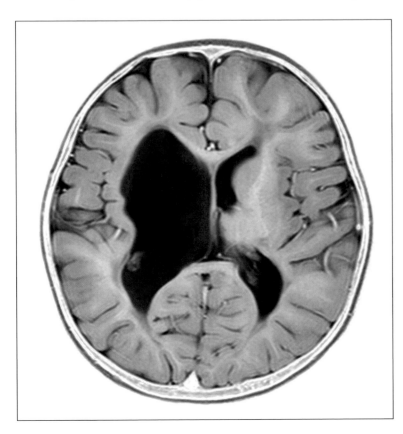

This magnetic resonance imaging scan shows a horizontal section of the head of a child with cerebral palsy. A porencephalic cyst filled with cerebrospinal fluid can be seen in dark blue. It has resulted in a left-sided weakness in the child. (**Simon Fraser/ Photo Researchers, Inc.**)

Silverman then started collaborating with Thomas Poulos, [Chancellor University] Professor of Molecular Biology and Biochemistry and a crystallographer from University of California, Irvine, who had been working on the structure of the neuronal brain enzyme. Silverman sent him several potent and selective compounds, and Poulos produced crystal structures showing each compound bound to the brain enzyme.

"Thanks to the talents of Tom and his associate Hui-ying Li we could, for the first time, see visually why these compounds were selective and also see the difference between them," said Silverman.

Haitao Ji, a postdoctoral fellow who is an expert in structure-based design, joined Silverman's team. Ji took the crystal structures of their molecules bound to the enzyme and, using computer modeling, designed new structures with even better properties.

These compounds were more potent and much more selective than earlier ones. Poulos produced crystal structures of the new compounds. These are the compounds that Tan tested on his cerebral palsy animal model with such promising results, as reported by the research team in the *Annals of Neurology* paper.

"This is a great example of a multi-institutional collaboration that could not have been done without each of the parts—we each contributed something different," said Silverman. "Science is going in that direction these days."

The researchers caution that taking the compounds to human clinical trials is a lengthy and complicated process. Silverman says they next plan to make the compounds even more potent, selective and bioavailable and then envision partnering with a company that would want to develop the drugs further.

Looking for a Genetic Cause for Cerebral Palsy

University of Adelaide

The following article discusses a landmark study designed by researchers at the University of Adelaide in Australia to look for a genetic cause for cerebral palsy. Beginning in 2008, researchers began collecting DNA from ten thousand mothers and their children. The researchers think that some infants may be genetically predisposed to cerebral palsy, and they hope to identify a gene or genes associated with the condition. According to the article, the researchers are hopeful that the results of their study will lead to the development of diagnostic tests or measures to prevent cerebral palsy. Since its establishment in 1874, the University of Adelaide has been among Australia's leading universities. The university is ranked in the top 1 percent in the world in eleven research fields.

Researchers from the University of Adelaide, Australia, have launched the largest study of its kind in the world in a bid to better understand the possible genetic causes of cerebral palsy.

SOURCE: University of Adelaide, "10,000 People in World-First Cerebral Palsy Study," July 2, 2008. Reproduced by permission.

The study—requiring cheek swabs of mothers and their children—aims to gather genetic samples from 10,000 people right across Australia.

One of the world's most serious complications during pregnancy and birth, cerebral palsy is a disability that affects one in every 500 children worldwide, and the consequences are life long.

Over the next two years [2008–2010] the researchers will test 5000 participants from families affected by cerebral palsy, while the other 5000 without an affected child will consist of a control group.

"Our study will investigate a key issue behind cerebral palsy: whether genetic factors make women more vulnerable to environmental risks that affect the brain of their unborn child. These risks—such as prematurity and infections—combined with genetic susceptibility mean that babies could be at double jeopardy of cerebral palsy," says research leader Professor Alastair MacLennan, Head of Obstetrics & Gynaecology at the University of Adelaide. PhD student Michael O'Callaghan is the national coordinator of the trial.

Cerebral Palsy May Have Genetic Link

"Recent studies by our group suggest that cerebral palsy may be associated with genetic and other mutations that may increase blood clotting within the brain," says Professor MacLennan, who is also head of the South Australian Cerebral Palsy Research Group, the world's leading research group into the causes of cerebral palsy.

"An association between cerebral palsy and different types of herpes virus infection—such as cold sores and chicken pox—has also been discovered in South Australian studies.

"The next step is to see if this is true in a much larger population, comparing the genetics of both mother and child," he says.

People with cerebral palsy lack control of their movement and posture as a result of brain injury in the neuromotor region. The symptoms vary greatly in severity, ranging from poor muscle co-ordination to quadriplegia.

Cerebral palsy is usually present from birth. The injury to the brain does not get worse over time.

"It was once thought that cerebral palsy was caused by low oxygen levels during birth. However, this is rarely the case," Professor MacLennan says.

Australian studies have found a possible link between cerebral palsy and different types of herpes simplex virus infections, such as cold sores, as shown here, and chicken pox. (Biophoto Associates/ Photo Researchers, Inc.)

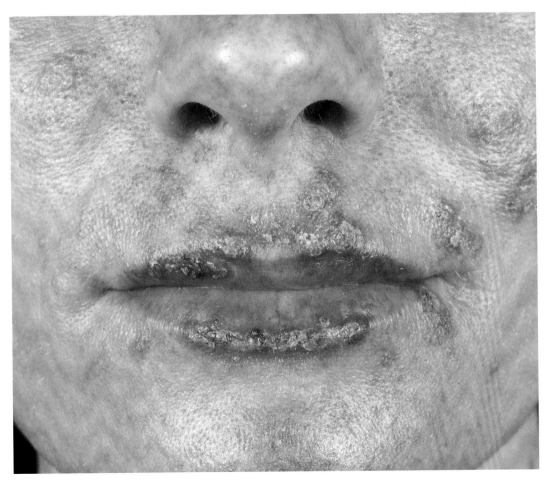

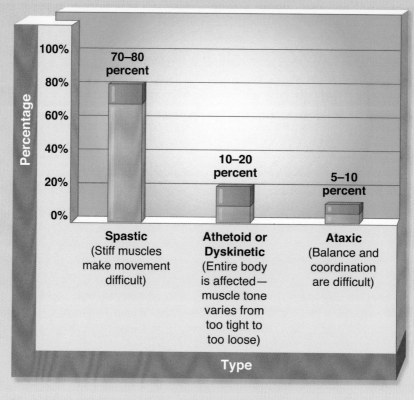

Types of Cerebral Palsy

Taken from: March of Dimes, 2007, www.marchofdimes.com/pnhec/4439_1208.asp.

"Obstetric care and caesarean deliveries have increased six-fold over the last 50 years, but the incidence of cerebral palsy cases has remained the same. Most of the cases are associated with problems during pregnancy and possible genetic susceptibility. Currently there is no cure or way to prevent cerebral palsy," he says.

"If our research confirms that there are genetic mutations that can lead to cerebral palsy, specific disease preventions may be available for individuals.

"In the future, gene therapy may allow doctors to alter the aberrant genes in a mother or fetus, or specific drugs could be used to counter the effect of genetic mutations and ultimately prevent a child from developing cerebral palsy before birth.

"Knowledge of a patient's genetic makeup and tailored administration of anti-inflammatory drugs before and during pregnancy may be possible. Immunisation against viral infections also may be a future option when this preventative therapy is available," he says.

Hypothermia May Help Prevent Cerebral Palsy

Elizabeth Fernandez

In the following selection Elizabeth Fernandez describes a relatively new treatment that may help prevent brain damage in newborns at risk of developing cerebral palsy or other neurological disorders. Fernandez presents the story of Nolan Hochleutner, who was at risk of developing cerebral palsy when his oxygen levels plunged to critical levels during his birth. Nolan's doctors rushed him off to the University of California–San Francisco where he was placed on a cooling blanket and kept at low temperatures for three days. Research suggests that the low temperature is protective of brain tissue. Nolan's parents are hopeful that the hypothermia treatment will prevent Nolan from developing cerebral palsy or other developmental disorders. Fernandez is a reporter for the *San Francisco Chronicle*.

T he pregnancy was normal. And for a dozen hours, the delivery at a South Bay [San Francisco] hospital seemed to be going smoothly, too.

SOURCE: Elizabeth Fernandez, "UCSF's Cooling Method a First for At-Risk Babies," *San Francisco Chronicle*, December 16, 2008. Copyright © 2008 Hearst Communications Inc., Hearst Newspaper Division. Reproduced by permission.

Then, in the span of 10 minutes, everything went horribly awry.

Nelya Hochleutner's uterus ruptured, and the birth of baby Nolan—whose heart rate and oxygen levels had plunged—suddenly became a critical emergency.

When he was born, his skin was blue and he needed resuscitation. Within an hour, he was having seizures.

"It felt like we had wakened to a nightmare," said the infant's father, Mike Hochleutner. "We had no idea what the future held for our son."

The doctors told him there was little they could do other than to continue to give Nolan anti-seizure medication. But, they said, UCSF [University of California–San Francisco] had a special new treatment that might help.

"Cooling" Intensive Care for Babies' Brains

With Hochleutner's consent, Nolan was rushed by ambulance to UCSF, and in a special intensive care unit there, was placed onto a cooling blanket that lowered his tiny body's core temperature in an effort to prevent or minimize the possibility of brain damage. And there, connected to a battery of monitors, Nolan would lie for three days.

The hypothermia treatment is part of a groundbreaking infant-care unit that recently opened at UCSF's Children's Hospital. The nation's first neuro-intensive care nursery, it offers specialized treatment for infants who show indications of brain damage at birth, which puts them at risk of developing cerebral palsy, mental retardation or other cognitive disorders.

The unit represents a new concept—to identify brain issues in newborns at a time when their medical conditions might still be reversed.

"It's really a baby brain ICU [intensive care unit]," said Dr. David Rowitch, chief of neonatology at the children's

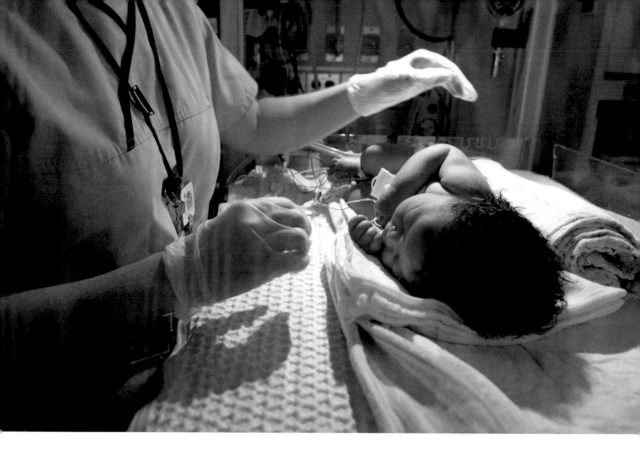

An infant lies on a cooling blanket during hypothermia treatment. By lowering his core body temperature, researchers hope to minimize the possibility of brain damage. (AP Images)

hospital who helped launch the unit. "The technical details of looking carefully at these babies turns out to be very complicated. You need very intensive monitoring and a lot of specialists."

Some of the infants in the unit had undergone a difficult delivery, suffering birth asphyxia. This condition can result in a range of hardships as the child grows, from mild learning problems to an inability to feed or breathe on one's own.

Other babies in the unit were born prematurely. As survival rates among preemies have increased, so has the rate of infants with cerebral palsy.

Rowitch says there's a direct link.

"The younger we go, the more vulnerable the brain is," he said.

The specialized unit is also focusing on babies who have suffered strokes—before, during delivery or immediately after delivery.

Approximately 1 in 2,300 babies experience a stroke, said Dr. Donna Ferriero, chief of pediatric neurology at the UCSF Children's Hospital and director of the Neonatal Brain Disorders Center. The causes include malformations of blood vessels, infection, or problems with blood clotting.

"That is equivalent to the number of strokes in the elderly," she said.

Going into Hibernation

While several medical centers offer hypothermia therapy, UCSF's neuronursery is the only one of its kind, combining such components as research, neuroradiology, infant care and therapy. So far, about 40 babies have undergone the treatment at UCSF. The babies are referred from hospitals throughout Northern California.

The hypothermia treatment was suggested from animal studies, said Rowitch.

"If you expose the animals to lack of oxygen, then cool their body a few degrees, they have better outcomes," he said. "We think it is only effective (among babies) within six hours of birth."

The babies lie on a special pad, much like a tiny raft. Circulating through the pad are coils containing water. The coils can be heated or cooled depending on medical need.

For three days, the baby's temperature is dropped to 92.3 Fahrenheit—normal temperature is 98.6. Then the baby is gradually warmed.

While on the blanket, the babies are put on a morphine-sulfate drip, which sedates them to minimize movement. They are fed through an IV. A urinary catheter is inserted as well as a rectal probe to monitor the baby's temperature. Three tiny probes are placed just under the babies' scalps connecting them to a monitor that records brain activity.

> **FAST FACT**
>
> According to Freeman Miller and Steven Bachrach in their book *Cerebral Palsy: A Complete Guide for Caregiving*, about 9 percent of children with cerebral palsy are thought to have it exclusively because of asphyxia at delivery.

"Cooling is so counter-intuitive to the way we think—you always want to keep a baby warm," said Susan Peloquin, the clinical coordinator of the neonatal ICU who wears a fleece vest adorned with a penguin to symbolize the treatment. "But once it's explained that it will help the brain, the fears of parents are allayed."

Mike Hochleutner said his little son went into hibernation.

Avoiding Later Developmental Problems

"When I first saw Nolan in the incubator, it looked like he was in a little rocket ship," he said. "He looked so damaged. The doctors told me that a year ago they wouldn't

Most Common Causes of Postnatal Cerebral Palsy

This graph indicates the most common causes of postnatal cerebral palsy affecting children who are at least thirty days old.

Taken from: Metropolitan Atlanta Developmental Disabilities Surveillance Program, 1991.
www.cdc.gov/mmwr/preview/mmwrhtml/00040247.htm#00001498.htm.

have had any treatment for him. They would have just had to let it run its course."

During the week Nolan was hospitalized, Mike Hochleutner hung a UCSF pennant near his son's incubator and bought himself a UCSF sweatshirt—a considerable gesture for a man who works as an administrator at Stanford University.

"I'm so proud of my son—at a week old, he graduated from an incredibly prestigious institution," said Hochleutner.

Nolan, who is regularly being monitored as part of ongoing UCSF research, is now 4 months old, weighs 14 pounds, and has just started teething. Big sister, Sofia, 5, loves to fetch things for him and to read him books. The Hochleutners hope that the cooling treatment at UCSF will prevent any ongoing developmental issues for him.

"There's no way to know at this point," Mike Hochleutner said. "Most problems you can see within a year. Some conditions don't manifest themselves until age 6 or beyond. But we are very hopeful. We haven't seen anything that causes us great concern."

"He seems completely normal," says Nelya Hochleutner, a stay-at-home mother. "He's a joyous little boy, he smiles all the time. We're so lucky that this treatment was around."

Robotic Therapy Holds Promise for Cerebral Palsy Patients

Anne Trafton

In the following article Anne Trafton discusses promising new robotic technology being developed by researchers at the Massachusetts Institute of Technology (MIT) that may help people with cerebral palsy. The robotic technology, which was initially developed for use with stroke patients, gently assists patients as they move objects. The technology is based on the premise that doing repetitive movements and thinking about doing them trigger dormant nerve cells in the brains of people with cerebral palsy. Trafton is a biology and life sciences writer for *MIT News*.

Over the past few years, MIT [Massachusetts Institute of Technology] engineers have successfully tested robotic devices to help stroke patients learn to control their arms and legs. Now, they're building on that work to help children with brain injuries and disorders such as cerebral palsy.

"Robotic therapy can potentially help reduce impairment and facilitate neuro-development of youngsters

SOURCE: Anne Trafton, "Robotic Therapy Holds Promise for Cerebral Palsy," *MIT News*, May 19, 2009. Reproduced by permission.

with cerebral palsy," says Hermano Igo Krebs, principal research scientist in mechanical engineering and one of the project's leaders.

Krebs and others at MIT, including professor of mechanical engineering Neville Hogan, pioneered the use of robotic therapy in the late 1980s, and since then the field has taken off.

Research Started with Stroke Patients

"We started with stroke because it's the biggest elephant in the room [i.e., the most pressing problem], and then started to build it out to other areas, including cerebral palsy as well as multiple sclerosis, Parkinson's disease and spinal cord injury," says Krebs.

The team's suite of robots for shoulder-and-elbow, wrist, hand and ankle has been in clinical trials for more than 15 years with more than 400 stroke patients. The Department of Veterans Affairs has just completed a large-scale, randomized, multisite clinical study with these devices.

All the devices are based on the same principle: that it is possible to help rebuild brain connections using robotic devices that gently guide the limb as a patient tries to make a specific movement.

When the researchers first decided to apply their work to children with cerebral palsy, Krebs was optimistic that it would succeed, because children's developing brains are more plastic than adults', meaning they are more able to establish new connections.

The MIT team is focusing on improving cerebral palsy patients' ability to reach for and grasp objects. Patients handshake with the robot via a handle, which is connected to a computer monitor that displays tasks similar to those of simple video games.

> **FAST FACT**
>
> According to the American Pregnancy Association, cerebral palsy usually is not diagnosed until a child is two to three years of age.

Approximate Costs for Cerebral Palsy Treatment and Equipment

Treatment and Equipment	Cost
Serial casting	$15,000
Physical therapy	$100–$280 per hour
Botox injections	$2,000
Baclofen pump	$23,000
Percutaneous muscle lengthening	$4,000
Ankle foot orthosis	$1,500
Adaptive bike	$2,500

Taken from: *Cerebral Palsy Magazine*, December 2006.

In a typical task, the youngster attempts to move the robot handle toward a moving or stationary target shown on the computer monitor. If the child starts moving in the wrong direction or does not move, the robotic arm gently nudges the child's arm in the right direction.

Krebs began working in robotic therapy as a graduate student at MIT almost 20 years ago. In his early studies, he and his colleagues found that it's important for stroke patients to make a conscious effort during physical therapy. When signals from the brain are paired with assisted movement from the robot, it helps the brain form new connections that help it relearn to move the limb on its own.

Even though a stroke kills many neurons, "the remaining neurons can very quickly establish new synapses or reinforce dormant synapses," says Krebs.

For this type of therapy to be effective, many repetitions are required—at least 400 in an hour-long session.

Cerebral Palsy Patients May Receive Lasting Benefits

Results from three published pilot studies involving 36 children suggest that cerebral palsy patients can also benefit from robotic therapy. The studies indicate that robot-mediated therapy helped the children reduce impairment and improve the smoothness and speed of their reaching motions.

The researchers applied their work to stroke patients first because it is such a widespread problem—about 800,000 people suffer strokes in the United States every year. About 10,000 babies develop cerebral palsy in the United States each year, but there is more potential for long-term benefit for children with cerebral palsy.

A patient uses a robotic arm, manipulating it with a joystick to maneuver a yellow dot through a maze. A few pilot studies seem to indicate that robotic therapy may be helpful for cerebral palsy patients. (**Pasquale Sorrentino/Photo Researchers, Inc.**)

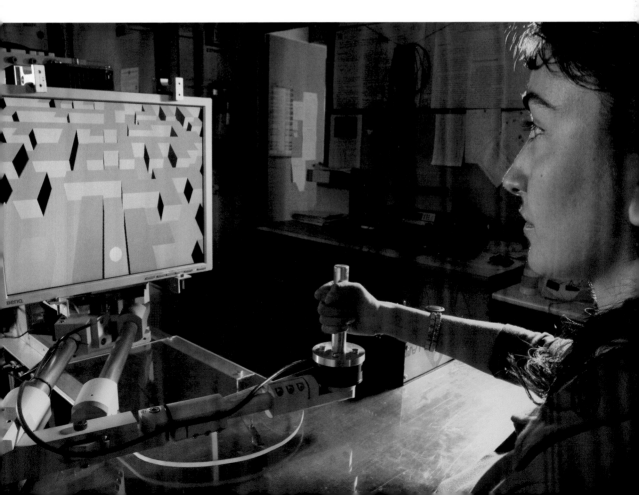

"In the long run, people that have a stroke, if they are 70 or 80 years old, might stay with us for an average of 5 or 6 years after the stroke," says Krebs. "In the case of cerebral palsy, there is a whole life."

Most of the clinical work testing the device with cerebral palsy patients has been done at Blythedale Children's Hospital in Westchester County, N.Y., and Spaulding Rehabilitation Hospital in Boston. Other hospitals around the country and abroad are also testing various MIT-developed robotic therapy devices.

Krebs' team has focused first on robotic devices to help cerebral palsy patients with upper body therapy, but they have also initiated a project to design a pediatric robot for the ankle.

CHAPTER 2

Controversies Surrounding Cerebral Palsy

Cord Blood Infusions Offer Hope for Babies with Cerebral Palsy

Bob Considine

In the following viewpoint Bob Considine presents the story of Dallas Hextell, a child whose cerebral palsy appears to have been alleviated by a transfusion of stem cells extracted from the stored blood of his umbilical cord. Dallas and his parents were interviewed on NBC's *Today* show regarding the use of cord blood to treat Dallas's cerebral palsy. According to his parents, saving the cord blood was a life-altering decision. They have seen dramatic and noticeable differences in Dallas since he received the cord blood transfusion. Considine is a contributor to *Today*'s Web site, Todayshow.com.

D allas Hextell was already a miracle to parents Cynthia and Derak, after they spent three years trying to get pregnant.

But now he is looking like a medical miracle to the rest of the world.

Photo on previous page. A close-up view of cryopreserved cord blood stem cells is shown here. The use of stem cells in cerebral palsy research is controversial. **(Chris Walker/MCT/Landov)**

SOURCE: Bob Considine, "Amazing Recovery Attributed to Cord Blood," *Today Health,* March 11, 2008. Copyright © 2010 MSNBC Interactive. Republished with permission of MSNBC.com, conveyed through Copyright Clearance Center, Inc.

The 2-year-old son of the Sacramento, Calif., couple was diagnosed with cerebral palsy [CP], but is now showing fewer signs of the disorder and marked improvement after an infusion of his own stem cells—made possible by the preservation of his own cord blood shortly before birth.

Derak Hextell now believes his son will be cured of the incurable malady.

"[Dallas' doctors] said by the age of 7, there may be no signs of cerebral palsy at all," Hextell told *Today* co-host Meredith Vieira while holding a curious Dallas on his lap. "So he's on his way, as far as we're concerned."

For Cynthia Hextell, the changes in Dallas just five days after the intravenous infusion of his cord blood cells are not coincidental.

"[He's changed] almost in every way you can imagine, just from five days afterwards saying 'mama' and waving," she said. "We just feel like right now he really connects with you.

"It just seemed like a fog was over him before, like he just really wasn't there. There was kind of, like a glaze in his eyes. Now, as you can see, you can't get anything past him."

A Difficult Start

The joy of Dallas' birth in 2006 was met with gradual heartbreak as he was unable to feed from his mother. He was constantly crying and rarely opened his eyes. At five months, Dallas had trouble balancing himself and his head was often cocked to one side.

The Hextells switched pediatricians when Dallas was eight months old and was diagnosed with cerebral palsy—a group of nonprogressive disorders that affect a person's ability to move and to maintain balance and posture.

Various studies show that the damage to the motor-control centers of the young, developing brain that causes

CP occurs during pregnancy, although there are smaller percentages of the disorder occurring during childbirth and after birth through the age of 3.

"I think it's important to remind people that cerebral palsy has to do with the motor part of the brain and usually kids don't deteriorate," said Dr. Nancy Snyderman, NBC News' chief medical editor. "But they have significant motor problems, which explains why he wasn't a good sucker when he was breast-feeding as a baby and all of this colicky stuff that sort of confused the diagnosis."

There is no known cure for cerebral palsy, and the treatments to help manage its debilitating effects make it the second-most expensive developmental disability to manage over a person's lifetime, behind mental disabilities.

At 18 months, Dallas had very limited motor skills. He could not crawl, clap or sit up and he communicated only through screaming brought on mostly by pain and frustration.

FAST FACT

According to the U.S. National Cord Blood Program, cord blood has been used in the treatment of more than seventy different diseases.

A Life-Changing Decision

During her pregnancy, Cynthia Hextell had done thorough Web research on health issues relating to childbirth and came across a pop-up ad for Cord Blood Registry, the world's largest family cord blood stem cell bank. The San Bruno, Calif.-based company has preserved cord blood stem cells for more than 200,000 newborns throughout the world.

Hextell said the cost of saving Dallas' cord blood—about $2,000 and not covered by insurance—was off-putting. But she ultimately registered for CBR, thinking she would rather put up the money and not use it rather than have saved it and regretted it later. . . .

"We had a perfectly healthy pregnancy, but it did take us three years to get pregnant," Cynthia Hextell told Vieira. "It was a good chance he was going to be our only child, so that was one thing that if we were going to do it, this was our only chance.

"Heart disease ran in [Derak's] family, I was adopted, so I knew if we ever needed something, Dallas and I were the only ones [who could provide a genetic match]. So those were things [we considered], but nothing like I thought something was going to be wrong with my child. Literally, it took us until about two weeks before our due date to make the final decision because it is expensive."

After Dallas was diagnosed, the Hextells traveled to Duke University, where doctors were using cord blood as part of a clinical trial to treat a small number of children who had cerebral palsy or brain damage. Mrs. Hextell called some of the parents of the children and all of them reported tangible improvement in their children following the transplant of stem cells, evidenced in better speech and motor skills.

A biotechnologist processes cord blood for stem cells. Stem cells are now being used to alleviate the effects of cerebral palsy. **(Luis Enrique Ascui/Reuters/Landov)**

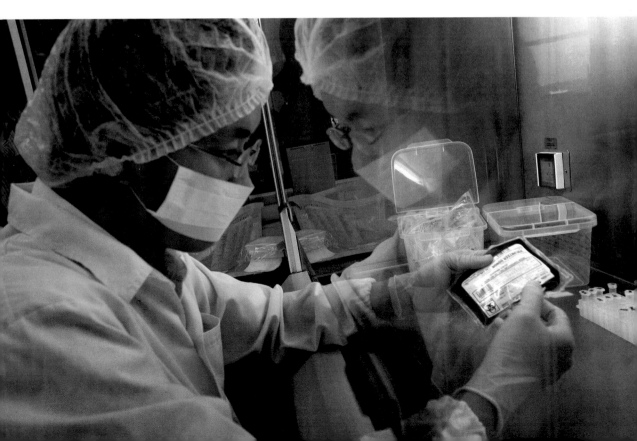

So the Hextells agreed to infuse Dallas' own stem cells back into his bloodstream, a procedure that took less than an hour.

Within five days, a different child emerged—laughing, clapping, waving and reacting.

"We think [the transfusion] has a real big part to do with it because it was such a drastic change within five days of the procedure taking place," Derak Hextell said. "It had to be because he wasn't reaching the milestones that he's reaching now. He was falling further and further behind."

"Before he went to Duke, we were trying to teach him to use a walker," Cynthia Hextell said. "Now he walks with no assistance at all."

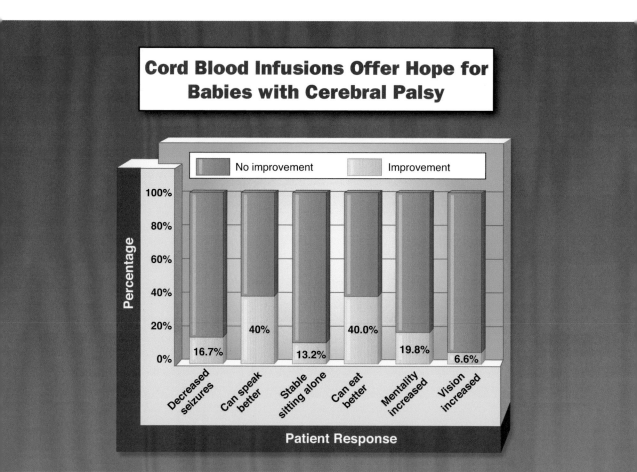

Taken from: "Stem Cell Treatment of Cerebral Palsy," X-Cell Center at the Institute for Regenerative Medicine.
www.xcell-center.com/treatments/diseases-treated/cerebral-palsy.aspx.

Saving the Cells

Although Dallas' case was not part of a controlled case study, Snyderman said it should not be overlooked in the progressing studies of stem cell treatments.

"I think the thing that medicine has not done very well is we haven't made a big enough deal about anecdotes," she said. "This is not a controlled case study. It's not a randomized clinical trial. But it is a child with a diagnosis who got a transfusion of stem cells and not only stopped the deterioration of his problems, [but] he's doing better.

"So I take it very seriously. And I think it's an extraordinary reminder that cord blood, that stuff that is thrown away with the placenta in the emergency room as a sort of medical waste, can have extraordinary applications. We're all offered it in the delivery room."

Snyderman didn't have to convince one person about the promise of those stem cells.

Said Cynthia Hextell: "They're like gold."

Claims That Cord Blood Infusions Cure Cerebral Palsy Are Exaggerated

Brenda Patoine

In the following viewpoint Brenda Patoine contends that the media exaggerate the benefits of stem cell treatments for cerebral palsy. According to Patoine, cord blood banks are using anecdotal stories, which are unscientific and subjective, to promote the use of their services. Patoine speaks with many scientists who say umbilical cord stem cells offer promise for treating cerebral palsy and other neurodegenerative disorders. "Miraculous cures," however, have not been seen. Patoine urges caution and patience until nonbiased scientific studies show the measurable effectiveness of umbilical cord stem cell treatments for cerebral palsy. Patoine is a science writer who writes regularly for the Dana Foundation and the *Annals of Neurology*.

The annals of medical history are littered with "miracle" treatments that defy scientific rationale or evidentiary standards, and the modern-day version often involves stem cells. But in today's environment

SOURCE: Brenda Patoine, "Media Focus on 'Miracle Cure' for Cerebral Palsy Pits Science vs. Hype," *Annals of Neurology,* October 2009, pp. A9–A11. Copyright © 2009 by American Neurological Association. This material is used by permission of John Wiley & Sons, Inc.

of 24-and-7 news and Web communications, it doesn't take long for the hype about a new therapeutic approach to get ahead of the science. Sometimes way ahead.

Just ask Joanne Kurtzberg, a cord-blood researcher at Duke University. She has just finished an open-label feasibility and safety trial for children with cerebral palsy [CP] from various etiologies [causes], in which the children's own cord blood, banked at birth, is infused intravenously. Kurtzberg has not yet published or presented any scientific results, and has been cautious in the few public statements she has made about the study.

Nevertheless, numerous local and national news programs have reported on a few children enrolled in the study whose parents have attributed dramatic changes in their child to the cell therapy. Many reports have sensationalized the stories. A July 2008 *Fox and Friends* interview with the parents of one child was slug-lined "Miracle Cure?" and used the word "miracle" or "miraculous" five times. An accompanying article on FOX News.com was headlined "Cord Blood Stem Cells Reverse Girl's Cerebral Palsy."

NBC's *Today Show* interviewed the parents of another child in the Duke study in a lengthy segment that also carried the title "Miracle Cure?" In it, NBC's chief medical editor Nancy Snyderman argued that such cases should not be overlooked just because they're not part of a randomized, controlled study, opining that "medicine has not . . . made a big enough deal about anecdotes."

These and dozens of similar stories, most focusing on the same few children, are recycled endlessly on YouTube, on Web blogs related to CP, and on the Web sites of the cord-blood banks that are referring parents to the Duke study. They are even being highlighted on some of the sponsored chat sites of many overseas "stem cell clinics" that are not involved in the Duke research but appear to be using the reports to justify stem cell–based treatments for CP.

"Hyped Up" Media Reports

Kurtzberg said the press attention has made her "insane." She said: "Some of the stuff that's been in the press about children who have been treated has definitely been hyped up, [and] some of the things that were reported to have happened, didn't." For example, one child was reported to not be able to walk before the treatment and to walk afterward, but Kurtzberg said, "That child was walking at the time we treated him."

She is convinced that private banks like Cord Blood Registry [CBR] and Viacord, based in Cambridge, Mass., have been behind a lot of the publicity surrounding her study.

"CBR and Viacord are using this as marketing tools," she said. "They have exploited our work and they have exploited parents. They are inappropriately promoting this procedure as successful, in the press and on their Web site."

She said changes that parents may notice within a few days post-infusion are unlikely to be due to the transplant. "It is really not possible for the cells themselves to make differences that quickly," she said. "These children are not static—sometimes things may have happened for real, but they should not have been attributed to the cells."

In some cases, she thinks there is "a big placebo effect" and "lots of wishful thinking" behind parental reports. "We do have some descriptive evidence that some kids' function is improving more than we would have predicted by certain neurodevelopment scales, but it's soft [data]; it's not hard."

Kurtzberg said the research has shown, in about 100 children, that IV [intravenous] administration of the autologous [self-donated] cord blood is safe and feasible. While there are "some hints that there may be some benefits," she emphasized that "it's very, very difficult to successfully assess efficacy."

Growing Demand

In the meantime, word of the Duke trial has spread fast in the CP patient/family community. Parents are going to great lengths—and reportedly incurring costs up to $15,000—to get on the Duke protocol. (The costs are typically borne by the family, though in some cases Duke waives its professional fees and/or the referring cord blood bank provides financial assistance.) "More patients are being treated because more families are hearing about this, some through the lay press and through these message boards and online [forums], and more doctors

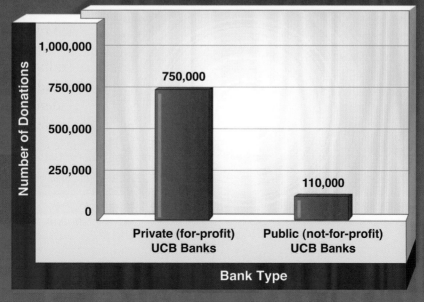

Donations to Private Versus Public Umbilical Cord Blood (UCB) Banks

In the United States, private umbilical cord blood banks receive more donations than public UCB banks, as of June 2008.

Taken from: Parents' Guide to Cord Blood Foundation, January 2010. www.parentsguidecordblood.org.

are hearing about it from patients who've gone [to Duke] and come back," said David Harris, a professor of immunobiology at the University of Arizona, Tucson who is affiliated with Cord Blood Registry (CBR), the largest private cord-blood bank and the source of autologous blood for many of the patients in the Duke study.

The University of Arizona [UA] is among a handful of institutions now moving forward with their own clinical programs using cord-blood transplantation in children with CP; UA treated the first child in May [2009]. Harris estimated that having the procedure in Tucson would cost about $4,000, which he said was about one-half to one-third the cost at Duke.

The Medical College of Georgia [MCG] is also starting a trial using autologous cord-blood to treat children with CP, according to MCG neurology chairman David Hess. . . .

And at the University of Texas–Houston, pediatric surgeon Charles Cox and pediatric neurosurgeon James Baumgartner are seeking FDA [Food and Drug Administration] approval for a study using autologous cord blood to treat acute brain-injured children, including children with CP. . . .

FAST FACT

Privately owned umbilical cord blood banks typically charge parents about one thousand to two thousand dollars to process a deposit of cord blood and a yearly storage fee thereafter.

The Rationale for Cord-Blood Transplants

Duke's transplant program has treated about 1,200 children with cancer or genetic diseases since the early 1990's. Kurtzberg, the program's director, said her hypothesis that autologous cord-blood transplants might be beneficial in children with CP is based on research using allogenetic [from nongenetically-related donors] cord-blood transplants for children with neurogenetic conditions. Her team published results in 2005 from 25 newborns with infantile Krabbe's disease [a rare, often fatal degenerative disorder that causes loss of the myelin sheath that surrounds nerve cells].

"In those children, we were able to show that donor cells could get into the brain, that remyelination could occur in demyelinating diseases, and that we could see improvement in neurologic disabilities, particularly when we transplanted early in the course of the disease," she said.

Evan Snyder, a neuroscientist and pediatric neurologist who heads the stem cell and regenerative medicine program at the Burnham Institute for Medical Research in La Jolla, Calif., said he thinks that umbilical cord blood cells can be "surprisingly useful" in some cases, including early treatment of lysosomal storage diseases, particularly Krabbe's disease. He said the work published by Kurtzberg and colleagues in the *New England Journal of Medicine* showed a "fairly impressive impact" in some children with these genetic diseases when cord-blood transplants were done very early, in the first couple weeks of life.

Snyder collaborated with Kurtzberg to conduct autopsies on some of the children who were transplanted. He said "very preliminary" unpublished data suggests that "the cells do make it through the blood-brain barrier, they will produce the missing enzyme . . . but they do not become nerve cells."

Kurtzberg pointed to an autopsy report from her own group, in which a child who was transplanted showed evidence of engrafted cells and remyelination in the brain, which led her to hypothesize that "we could grow oligodendrocytes [a type of brain cell] from cord blood."

Snyder said the idea that umbilical cord cells can make oligodendrocytes "is exceptionally controversial. Given how controversial it is, I don't know whether one should predicate a clinical trial based on those data." . . .

"Tremendous Potential" for Harm

Stephen Back, a pediatric neurologist and research scientist at Oregon Health Sciences University who studies mechanisms of white matter [brain tissue] disease, including models of neonatal hypoxia-ischemia [inadequate oxygenation due to restricted blood flow], said it is still "very unclear" how these injuries evolve from one stage to another. He said many basic questions need to be answered "before you start marching in and giving therapy for kids with CP.

"It frightens me to think of something like that without understanding what the pathogenesis [origination and development] of the disorder is," Back said. "There is tremendous hesitancy on the part of the world medical community to initiate a stem cell trial in a nonfatal, nonprogressive disorder like CP. There is always a tremendous potential to do harm."

A member of a transplant team checks on a fourteen-month-old recipient of a cord blood transplant. The treatment has become highly controversial. (Tammy Ljungblad/MCT/ Landov)

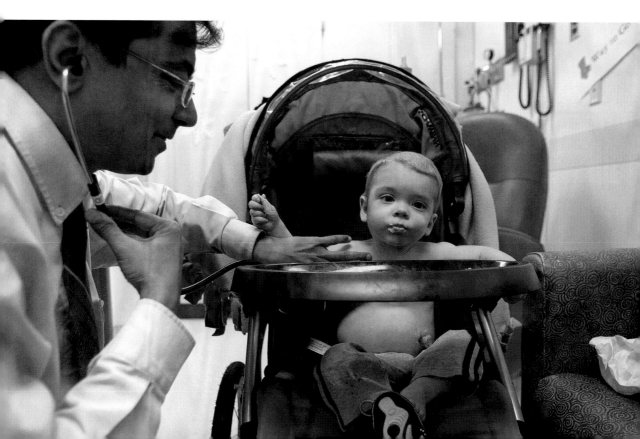

The first two FDA-approved stem cell trials in this country, which use neural stem cells, are being conducted in children with progressive, invariably fatal conditions: Batten disease and Pelizaeus-Merzbacher disease.

Steven Levison, a neuroscientist who directs the Laboratory of Regenerative Neurobiology at the University of Medicine & Dentistry of New Jersey in Newark, shares Back's concerns about cord-blood treatment for CP: "I think there is a lot more that we need to know. There is not enough in the published literature in terms of preclinical models of people putting in umbilical cord blood cells.

"I do think it is worth evaluating, because there have been lots of studies that suggest that stem cells can modify the brain after injury and promote behavioral recovery," he said. "As far as I can tell, the use of umbilical cord cells is safe—they've been used in lots of other diseases—so there may be no harm done. But there needs to be some additional evidence and unbiased studies that are done to evaluate the efficacy of these cells."

Kurtzberg is seeking stimulus funding for a randomized, placebo-controlled trial to "really see if the cells are benefiting these kids.

"We really have to have nonbiased studies that are not influenced by any level of support by any private bank," she said.

Fetal Monitoring Can Help Prevent Cerebral Palsy

Howard A. Janet

In the following viewpoint Howard A. Janet contends that electronic fetal monitoring can prevent cerebral palsy in many births. According to Janet, a significant percentage of cerebral palsy cases are caused by "intrapartum asphyxia," a condition in which a newborn suffers from lack of oxygen during the birth process. Electronic fetal monitors measure a fetus's heart rate and can alert doctors to when a fetus is in danger of intrapartum asphyxia. Doctors can then act to alleviate the fetal distress and ensure that oxygen and blood flow are adequate. Janet says there is a great deal of misinformation surrounding electronic fetal monitoring, but he hopes more physicians and health-care practitioners will speak out about its benefits and that more parents will become educated on the use of this important technique that can prevent cerebral palsy. Janet is an attorney in the law firm Janet, Jenner, and Suggs, which specializes in birth injury litigation.

SOURCE: Howard A. Janet, "How Electronic Fetal Monitoring Can Prevent Cerebral Palsy," *Cerebral Palsy Magazine,* December 2005, pp. 60–63. Copyright © 2005 by Cerebral Palsy Magazine. Reproduced by permission.

The intent of this article is to help parents better understand issues surrounding one cause of cerebral palsy [CP]—oxygen deprivation during labor (intrapartum asphyxia), which can lead to brain injury. A lot of conflicting information is available about the prevalence of intrapartum asphyxia, how to prevent it and how to lower the risks of its occurring in future pregnancies.

There is a myth that intrapartum asphyxia is rare—a myth that has its roots in outdated research that has been disproved in recent years. And there is a second myth that electronic fetal monitoring (EFM) is an unreliable way to assess the well-being of fetuses during labor, and therefore, it doesn't help reduce the incidence of CP. The research and opinions of many respected physicians tell a different story.

The Importance of Learning About EFM

By learning more about EFM, parents can make an informed judgment about whether this technique was used properly during the labor and delivery of their own child. More importantly, those armed with this information can take knowledgeable, proactive steps to not only ensure the safe, healthy delivery of their next baby, but may also help ensure the baby of a friend or acquaintance has the same chance of good health.

Let me be clear: CP can be prevented in many births. We don't have to wait for medical science to find a way to prevent every CP occurrence. We can save many babies from developing this heartbreaking, debilitating condition today. Brain injuries during the intrapartum period that result from decreased oxygenated blood flow to the fetus often can be detected through accurate interpretation of EFM tracings and prevented by timely, appropriate action.

A problematic EFM pattern may require something as simple as giving intravenous fluids or oxygen to the

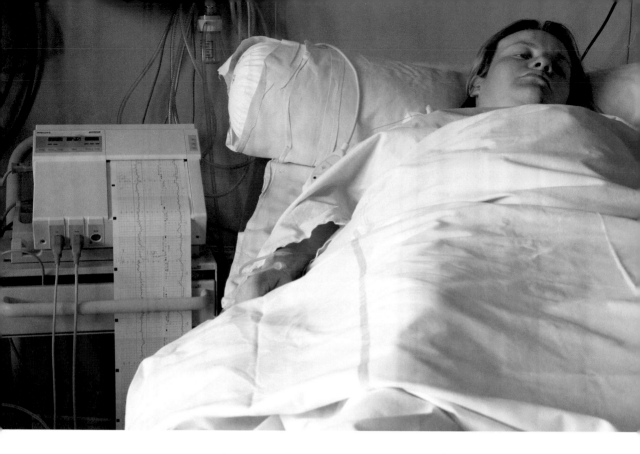

A large percentage of cerebral palsy cases occur when a fetus suffers from a lack of oxygen during the birth process. Fetal monitoring may help prevent the condition. **(BSIP/Photo Researchers, Inc.)**

mother, turning or repositioning her, discontinuing pushing, or stopping the administration of Pitocin (intrauterine resuscitative measures). On the other hand, certain EFM tracings may require more serious action, including an emergency Caesarean section.

Generally speaking, the public is unaware of electronic fetal monitoring issues. Soon-to-be parents devour every bit of information they can find about prenatal nutrition, exercise, birthing centers and labor techniques. However, they often have no understanding of the critical role that electronic fetal monitoring can play in the outcome of their delivery.

Just as parents are encouraged to enroll in Lamaze-type classes to learn how to ease the pain of labor and delivery, every parent also should be schooled in the meaning of certain EFM patterns. It is important for parents to know enough about EFM to be aware of the right questions to ask their obstetrician and labor room nurses about their baby's EFM tracings and how they relate to events that may occur during labor.

Knowledge Is Power

Generally, though, parents don't seek, nor are they encouraged to learn this kind of information. When it comes to getting the facts about how doctors and nurses use EFM tracings to monitor fetuses during labor and delivery, and the proper responses to those tracings, parents are encouraged to rely on their health care providers.

Unfortunately, health care providers themselves are divided on this issue, the result being that a lot of conflicting information—even misinformation—is generated. For example, even official obstetrical documents, such as *Practice Bulletin No. 62*, published by the American College of Obstetricians and Gynecologists (ACOG), contain inaccurate data and downplay the prevalence of cerebral palsy caused by intrapartum asphyxia, which in some instances is preventable.

In fact, so much outdated research data and distorted information is in circulation that it drowns out the voices of anyone who tries to call attention to data that proves EFM can prevent many cases of cerebral palsy. The truth about EFM is so buried in misleading medical literature that parents seeking an accurate, complete picture must dig deep to find it.

Conflicting Agendas

Popularized in the 1970s, EFM is a method for examining the condition of an unborn infant in the uterus by noting unusual patterns in its heart rate. EFM is a dependable measure of how the unborn child is withstanding the changes in environment and stimuli that it experiences during the birthing process. By monitoring the baby's heart rate and graphing it on strips of paper, called "tracings," doctors and labor room nurses have a

Normal Results from a Fetal Monitor Strip

This sample monitor strip shows the tracing of the fetal heart rate pattern at the top and the mother's contraction pattern at the bottom. The contractions are represented by the peaks in the lower pattern. The heart rate is in the normal range, and there are intermittent accelerations that occur when the baby moves. There are no decelerations in response to the contractions. If the fetal heart rate dipped after each contraction, especially if it fell below the normal heart-rate range, it would suggest oxygen deprivation and fetal distress.

Fetal Heart Rate During Normal Labor

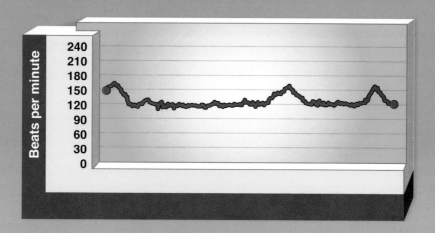

Mother's Contraction Pattern

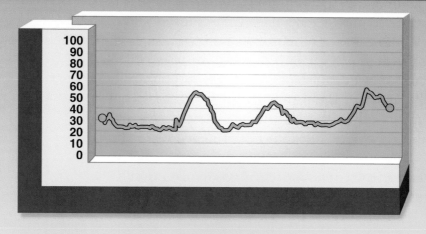

Taken from: Amy B. Tuteur, *How Your Baby Is Born*. Emeryville, CA: Ziff-Davis, 1994.

real-time, and an overall, picture of the baby's condition throughout labor.

Statistics compiled for the year 2002 indicate that EFM was used to monitor 85 percent of all births in United States hospitals. Many of the other 15 percent involved natural childbirth, where the parents opted to use midwives or to deliver their children in birthing centers. Even in natural settings, however, when a troublesome heart rate pattern develops during labor, those assisting with the birth usually move the mother immediately to a facility where EFM is available.

So, why would the medical community refute the reliability of EFM in publications and statements, while using it so widely and consistently?

Unfortunately, many in the medical field have an agenda that focuses more on shielding themselves or their colleagues from accountability than with educating patients and reducing the risk of CP.

Clearly, their concerns are misguided. These physicians and organizations should be a beacon of truth and knowledge for their patients. They should be a source of facts for patients and, indeed, a fountainhead of leading-edge information for parents who want to be proactive in their health care.

But a growing number of well-credentialed obstetricians, labor and delivery nurses, and midwives are speaking up. These preeminent members of the medical community, who use EFM every day to assess the well-being of fetuses during labor, say that EFM is viable and effective in reducing the incidence of CP, and fetal mortality as well. The efficacy of EFM is demonstrated further by the continuous increase in the percentage of births in which it is used: 45 in 1980, 62 in 1988, 74 in 1992, and 85 in 2002.

Fact Versus Fiction

Parents must realize that their quest for knowledge about their children's health care should start before the labor and delivery process. When you undertake your research, you will be astounded by the misinformation you will find. For instance:

Misinformation: Children rarely develop CP from asphyxial injuries to the brain during the intrapartum period. The American College of Obstetricians and Gynecologists claims that several studies support the conclusion that only four percent of CP results solely from asphyxia during labor.

Reality: The studies on which ACOG relied are inferior and unreliable. Even if the scope of the inquiry were limited to instances of CP where intrapartum asphyxia is the sole cause as opposed to the primary cause, the actual percentage would be approximately three times greater. According to Joseph J. Volpe, M.D., a Harvard professor and Neurologist-in-Chief at Boston's Children's Hospital, if all term infants are considered, the percentage of children who develop CP from intrapartum asphyxia is "approximately 12 to 23 percent" which equates to "a large absolute number of infants." Dr. Volpe concludes, further, that the "tendency in the medical profession to deny the importance or even the existence of intrapartum brain injury" is "particularly unfortunate," and may well be impairing progress in CP prevention.

Misinformation: Electronic fetal monitoring has not reduced the number of children who develop cerebral palsy.

Reality: This false claim fails to take into account today's enhanced survival rates of premature infants. Nationally renowned maternal-fetal medicine specialist, Richard H. Paul, M.D. (who is one of the pioneers in EFM), and other experts have testified to the inaccuracy of this claim in malpractice trials brought by parents who contend that their children's cerebral palsy was caused by medical error.

In the days before EFM and recent medical advancements, doctors lacked the expertise and technology to save many premature babies; generally, efforts made to save infants weighing less than three pounds were tragically unsuccessful. Today, infants of a pound or less receive active treatment and life support, and routinely survive. These premature infants represent a substantial number of the children born with CP. Yet, despite the addition of these preemies to the survival pool, the total number of infants born with CP has remained constant.

If the number of surviving premature babies who develop CP has significantly increased, but the total number of cases of CP remains the same, then the number of full-term infants that have CP must have declined. Many infants who otherwise might have developed CP have escaped an unfortunate fate because EFM was used properly during labor and delivery.

Misinformation: Obstetricians disagree so widely in their interpretation of EFM tracings that standards for interpretation and appropriate action in response to a particular EFM pattern do not exist except in the face of tracings that are perfectly normal or extremely and obviously abnormal. This contention is primarily based on three studies.

Reality: These studies are unpersuasive and outdated, with one being more than 23 years old and each involving no more than five obstetricians. For many years, highly qualified obstetricians from all over the country have testified in medical malpractice cases that standards of care indeed do exist for the interpretation and management of various EFM tracing patterns that fall between those two extremes.

When EFM patterns provide evidence of impending fetal asphyxia, such patterns need not reach the extremely abnormal level before immediate action, such as expedited Caesarean delivery must be taken. Yet, because medically sanctioned literature suggests that less-than-extreme EFM tracings don't necessarily require intervention, many otherwise healthy babies sustain intrapartum brain injuries and are subsequently diagnosed with

CP. In connection with a medical malpractice lawsuit brought by a Minnesota mother whose child developed CP as a result of intrapartum asphyxia, a medical article was uncovered that shed light on at least one reason why doctors resist establishing written standards for the interpretation and management of the so-called in between patterns. "Providers have traditionally been hesitant to codify guidelines for managing FHR [fetal heart rate] pattern tracings. The reasons commonly cited include . . . fears that written guidelines will be used to scrutinize clinical practice in a court of law."

More Misguided Priorities

As much as parents would like to believe that the best interests of mother and baby are always the first priority of the doctors and nurses who treat them, unfortunately, other considerations possibly come into play. According to the Association of Women's Health, Obstetrics and Neonatal Nurses (AWHONN), nurses may hesitate to document a physician's conduct in the medical record for fear those notes will end up in the courtroom: "[Nurses] are usually told by risk management personnel not to 'advertise' potential conflicts in the medical records and thus some nurses may be unwilling to memorialize an unsuccessful interaction with a physician. . . . Nurses may choose to affirmatively protect the doctor by not documenting an inappropriate or untimely response in the patient's chart."

Once parents . . . learn that even a publication of a professional nursing organization notes that its members are cautioned against documenting potential medical errors, [they] will realize the gravity of this matter and the importance of researching these issues.

A Call to Action

Significant numbers of highly qualified, respected physicians have concluded that many cases of cerebral palsy can be prevented through the judicious use of electronic fetal monitoring. Their positions are supported by recent medical studies that have established a distinct relationship between certain fetal heart rate patterns and poor neurological outcomes in infants up to a year after birth.

And while there may be no universally agreed upon set of terms to describe actionable EFM pattern characteristics, it is clear that doctors know a great deal about the patterns that foreshadow CP and other poor neonatal outcomes. By using EFM in 85 percent of all labor and delivery rooms nationwide, the medical community already has acknowledged EFM's value. Now, medical leaders should take action to adopt clear-cut written protocols concerning the interpretation of EFM tracings and appropriate interventions. Doing so will help reduce the number of errors made in connection with interpreting and responding to EFM tracings.

Health care organizations that promote better patient care should develop formalized classes and seminars that focus not only on easing the mother's pain, but also on educating parents-to-be about EFM and other matters that will help them be proactive in their health care.

These are complex, technical subjects, and some may be difficult to research, but accurate information is available. There really are standards, even if they have not been reduced to writing or codified by the obstetrical community. . . . Parents must do the research necessary to learn more about EFM and its value in the labor and delivery rooms. Remember, knowledge is power.

FAST FACT

According to the Centers for Disease Control and Prevention, developmental disabilities, such as cerebral palsy, affect approximately 17 percent of children younger than eighteen years of age in the United States.

Whether Fetal Monitoring Is Beneficial or Harmful Is Unclear

Jane Brody

In the following viewpoint Jane Brody discusses the controversy that exists over the benefits of electronic fetal monitors and whether they do more harm than good. Brody contends that doctors have a difficult time interpreting the tracings produced by the monitors, which measure a fetus's heart rate during labor. This difficulty has led to an increase in caesarean sections and in the use of forceps to quickly pull babies out of the womb by doctors fearful of being sued for malpractice. Additionally, claims Brody, fetal monitoring would not significantly reduce the overall risk of cerebral palsy because very few cases result from the birth process. According to Brody, physicians are hopeful that revised guidelines issued by the American College of Obstetrics and Gynecology in 2009 will help doctors better interpret fetal monitoring results and make more-informed decisions about the best delivery process for newborn babies. Brody is the author of several books and is the Personal Health columnist for the *New York Times*.

SOURCE: Jane Brody, "Updating a Standard: Fetal Monitoring," *New York Times,* July 7, 2009. Copyright © 2009 by The New York Times Company. Reproduced by permission.

Electronic fetal monitoring during labor and delivery was introduced into obstetrical practice in the early 1970s in hopes that it would reduce the risk of cerebral palsy and death resulting from inadequate oxygen to the fetal brain.

The monitors continually measure the fetal heart rate and produce tracings on a screen and paper that can alert a doctor to a baby who is doing poorly under the stress of labor. It is up to the doctor to try to alleviate the problem and, if those measures do not help, to decide whether to deliver the baby vaginally with forceps or surgically by Caesarean.

Negative and Positive Results

Today, more than 85 percent of the four million babies born alive in this country each year are assessed by electronic fetal monitoring, amid continuing controversy over whether it does more harm than good. New guidelines on fetal monitoring, published [in July 2009], aim to bring more consistency to how doctors interpret the results and act on them.

"Honestly, the technology got rolled out before we knew if it worked or not," Dr. George A. Macones, an obstetrician at Washington University in St. Louis, said in an interview.

Continuous monitoring became a standard obstetrical procedure before studies could show if the benefits outweighed the risks, and without clear-cut guidelines on how doctors should interpret the findings.

But experts report that the use of fetal monitoring has produced both negative and positive results, including these:
- Electronic monitoring has led to a significant increase in both Caesarean deliveries and forceps vaginal deliveries.
- Monitoring results are widely used by lawyers to bolster malpractice cases of spurious merit, which

has led to soaring costs for malpractice insurance and, in turn, prompted many obstetricians to stop delivering babies.

- Electronic monitoring has not reduced the risk of either cerebral palsy or fetal deaths.

Revised Guidelines Issued

[In 2008] a workshop held by the Eunice Kennedy Shriver National Institute of Child Health and Human Development produced new recommendations that have now been incorporated into revised practice guidelines by the American College of Obstetricians and Gynecologists and published in the July [2009] issue of the journal

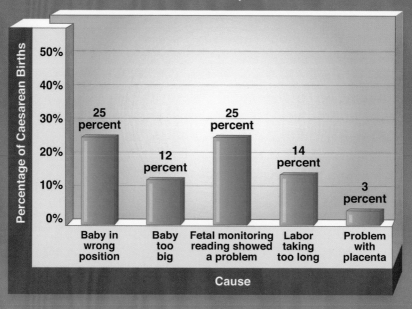

Fetal Monitoring Is Primary Reason for Caesarean Delivery

This graph illustrates the results of a 2006 survey of mothers whose babies were born via caesarean delivery.

Taken from: Eugene R. Declerq et al. *Listening to Mothers II: Report of the Second National U.S. Survey of Women's Childbearing Experiences.* New York: Childbirth Connection, October 2006.

Obstetrics & Gynecology. Dr. Macones supervised the development of the new guidelines.

The college hopes the revised guidelines will reduce misinterpretations and inconsistencies in the understanding and use of readings on fetal monitors, although experts are not optimistic that the rate of Caesareans will drop.

In cities like New York, Philadelphia and Chicago, as many as 40 percent of babies are delivered by Caesarean. Although it is one of the safest operations, it is not without risk to either mother or baby, and it is far more costly than a natural vaginal delivery.

Nor is it likely that any change in the use of monitors will result in a decrease in babies with cerebral palsy.

As the new practice bulletin explains, monitoring the fetus during labor does not affect the risk of cerebral palsy, because 70 percent of cases occur before labor begins and only 4 percent result solely from a mishap during labor and delivery. The remaining 26 percent of cases can be attributed to a combination of factors that occur before and during labor or after delivery, according to Dr. Macones and other experts who helped develop the guidelines.

> **FAST FACT**
>
> It is estimated that about eighty out of one hundred children with cerebral palsy had a disruption in the normal development of parts of their brain during fetal growth, according to WebMD.

Inconsistent Interpretations

How the new guidelines might affect the rate of malpractice cases is unknown. "Lawyers pick through every finding on the tracings and say the doctor should have done a Caesarean here and saved the baby," Dr. Macones said, "even though that's seldom the case since most cases of cerebral palsy don't happen during labor."

Doctors differ greatly in how they interpret tracings. In a study in which four obstetricians examined 50 fetal heart rate tracings, they agreed in 22 percent of the cases. Two months later, the same four doctors re-evaluated the same 50 tracings and changed their interpretations on nearly one of every five. Furthermore, when the baby's outcome is already known, interpretation of the tracings is especially unreliable, the guideline report says.

And in more than 99 percent of cases, predictions based on the tracings that the baby would have cerebral palsy have proved wrong.

Three Categories of Tracings Instead of Two

The new guidelines refine the meaning of different readings from the monitors, in the hopes of helping doctors make better decisions during labor about when to intervene and when to let nature take its course.

Previous guidelines divided readings into two categories—reassuring and nonreassuring—and it was up to the doctor to decide whether a nonreassuring reading meant the fetus was at serious risk of oxygen deprivation.

With fear of liability hanging over doctors' heads, many babies with "nonreassuring" readings who might have done just fine with a natural vaginal delivery are being delivered surgically or with forceps, Dr. Macones said.

The new guidelines divide monitor readings into three categories and help to make "the gray zone of nonreassuring clearer," Dr. Catherine Y. Spong, chief of the Pregnancy and Perinatology Branch at the child health institute, said in an interview.

In Category I, tracings of the fetal heart rate are normal and no specific action is required.

In Category II, indeterminate tracings require evaluation and continuous surveillance and re-evaluation, the guidelines say. Dr. Spong said that in deciding how serious the tracings are, doctors "need to look at the entire clinical picture, not just the tracing," and consider factors like the mother's blood pressure, heart rate and temperature, what medicines she might have been given,

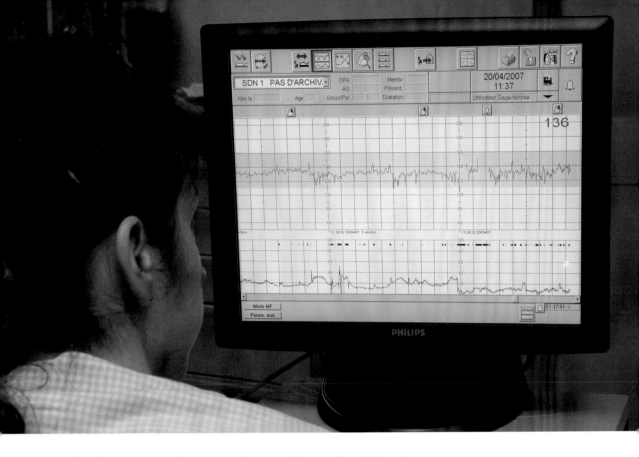

the frequency of contractions and how fast labor is progressing.

Depending on what makes the reading Category II, the doctor can take steps to see if the reading will go back to Category I, Dr. Spong said. For example, the doctor might try to stimulate the baby by scratching its scalp or making a loud noise, to see if the heart rate will accelerate naturally and bring the baby back to Category I.

Babies with Category II readings are not considered in danger, she said, "but they have to be watched very closely because they could become compromised."

In Category III, tracings are clearly abnormal, requiring prompt evaluation and efforts to reverse the abnormal heart rate. That could involve giving the mother oxygen, changing her position, treating her low blood pressure and stopping stimulation of labor if that is being done. If the tracing does not improve with such measures, the new guidelines say that "delivery should be undertaken."

A technician checks a fetal monitor to review the fetus's heart rhythm (top) and the rhythm of the mother's uterine contractions (bottom). (**BSIP/Photo Researchers, Inc.**)

Botox Treatments for Cerebral Palsy Are Risky

Lisa Girion

In the following viewpoint Lisa Girion asserts that using Botox to treat cerebral palsy is risky. Botox is made from the botulinum toxin—one of the most potent toxins in the world. The medical community has found many beneficial uses for the toxin, the most well known being to relax facial muscles, which reduces wrinkles. But doctors also use it to reduce spasticity, or muscle tightness, in people with cerebral palsy. Girion reports, however, that Botox may have caused the death of at least one young child suffering from cerebral palsy. She also asserts that the maker of Botox may have known about the dangers of the treatment before the child's death occurred. Girion is a writer for the *Los Angeles Times*.

Kristen Spears started getting Botox injections at the age of 6—not to smooth furrows in her brow but to calm spasms in her legs.

Kristen was born with severe cerebral palsy, and Botox, best known as a face-lift-in-a-syringe, can relax con-

SOURCE: Lisa Girion, "Case Raises Questions About Use of Botox to Treat Children with Cerebral Palsy," *Los Angeles Times,* January 28, 2010. Copyright © 2010 Los Angeles Times. Reproduced by permission.

torted muscles and sometimes help young patients walk without surgery.

Instead, Kristen's mother [Dee Spears] alleges, an overdose of the drug killed her.

Opening arguments in Spears' lawsuit are set to begin Wednesday [February 3, 2010,] in Orange County, Calif. At issue is the safety of Botox, especially in the higher dosages used to treat children with cerebral palsy. It is believed to be the first case to reach trial alleging a fatal reaction to the blockbuster drug, and is one of several pending suits related to its cosmetic and non-cosmetic uses.

Manufacturer Was Aware of Problems

The trial comes less than a year after federal authorities mandated "black box" labels warning of potentially serious reactions to Botox. And it opens a window on the Irvine, Calif.–based drug maker's own records of reported ill-effects, showing that the company knew of some serious problems linked to neurotoxins such as Botox as early as 2005.

Botox maker Allergan declined to comment on the trial. In a court motion, Allergan says Kristen died of a bacterial infection and that her mother cannot prove Botox killed her.

When the suit was filed, a spokeswoman characterized the drug's safety record as "remarkable." Serious side effects, she said, were rarely reported in more than 15 million treatments over two decades. In a confidential 2008 report to federal regulators, Allergan said it found that the risk of death among children with cerebral palsy was low and that fatalities often resulted from underlying poor health.

Approved in the U.S. specifically to treat frown lines, crossed eyes and other conditions, Botox yields $1.3 billion in annual sales. But the drug can be legally prescribed in the U.S. at doctors' discretion for a variety of other

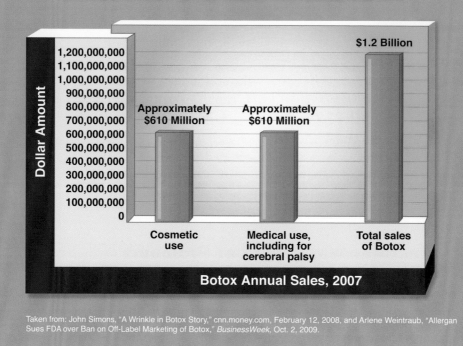

Botox Is a Billion-Dollar Market

Dollar Amount

1,200,000,000	
1,100,000,000	
1,000,000,000	
900,000,000	
800,000,000	
700,000,000	
600,000,000	
500,000,000	
400,000,000	
300,000,000	
200,000,000	
100,000,000	
0	

Approximately $610 Million — Cosmetic use

Approximately $610 Million — Medical use, including for cerebral palsy

$1.2 Billion — Total sales of Botox

Botox Annual Sales, 2007

Taken from: John Simons, "A Wrinkle in Botox Story," cnn.money.com, February 12, 2008, and Arlene Weintraub, "Allergan Sues FDA over Ban on Off-Label Marketing of Botox," *BusinessWeek*, Oct. 2, 2009.

purposes, including cerebral palsy. It is also specifically approved for cerebral palsy in many other countries. Its use for that condition alone contributed $47 million to Allergan's bottom line in 2007.

The drug uses botulinum toxin, a powerful poison, to block neural communications, allowing muscles that produce worry lines or gnarled limbs to relax. A few injections smooth wrinkles, while larger doses are required to relax arms and legs.

Kristen Spears died in November 2007 of respiratory failure and pneumonia, according to her death certificate. Experts hired by Dee Spears say Botox weakened muscles that controlled her breathing and swallowing, leading to respiratory failure and pneumonia.

Kristen's death came more than a year before the U.S. Food and Drug Administration [FDA] ordered the labels warning of the drug's potential to cause botulism symptoms, including "potentially life-threatening swallowing and breathing difficulties and even death."

At the same time, the agency required Allergan to notify physicians that the toxin could spread beyond the injection site and to prepare a patient guide saying it was not known whether Botox was safe for children or for other patients whose conditions it had not been approved to treat.

Spears alleges that Allergan knew problems had been reported at least two years before Kristen died. What's more, she alleges, Allergan encouraged Kristen's pediatrician to treat cerebral palsy patients with Botox and helped with his training.

"I don't want this to happen to anyone else's child," she said in a statement.

Confidential Reports

In preparation for the trial, Allergan was required to produce safety assessments of Botox and other confidential internal reports. Portions of some documents were obtained by the *Los Angeles Times* after Orange County Superior Court Judge Ronald L. Bauer unsealed them.

The documents include a 2005 letter sent by a European health official alerting Allergan of reports that botulinum toxin had spread beyond the injection site among patients who sought cosmetic treatment. There was at least one similar drug manufactured by another company in the European market, and the letter did not specify which products the reports related to.

Trouble with swallowing and "aspiration [sucking food or fluids into the lungs] have been reported to occur secondary to muscle weakness in the muscles in the neck region," the letter says. "Fatal cases of aspiration have been reported." In a confidential response dated Sept. 16, 2005, Allergan said its internal database contained 436 "serious

> **FAST FACT**
>
> According to the National Institute for Neurological Disorders and Stroke, the relaxing effects of a Botox injection usually last about three months.

adverse event" reports related to Botox. Of those, 201 were "serious, health care professional–confirmed cases with events possibly due to remote spread of the toxin," including 42 after facial wrinkle treatments.

Also in 2005, documents show, Allergan sent a confidential report to the FDA, saying an analysis identified 38 patients—20 children, most of them with cerebral palsy, and 18 adults—who had suffered seizures after Botox injections.

In May 2007, European regulators asked Allergan and two competitors to add information to labels and warn doctors that the toxin could spread, causing botulism symptoms.

Two months later, on July 16, 2007, consulting firm BioSoteria Inc., in a confidential report to Allergan, identified 207 patients with medical problems, including several deaths, associated with the spread of the toxin.

Allergan Corporation, which manufactures Botox, has been sued over the dangers of their product. The company knew of serious neurotoxic problems with Botox as early as 2005. **(AP Images)**

A third of the cases identified by BioSoteria occurred in people treated for wrinkles; the rest were treated for muscle spasms, muscle spasticity and eye problems. Proportionally more problems were reported among children.

Kristen's care proceeded as such reports flowed into Allergan, according to depositions and documents filed in court.

Questions About Dosage

The Amarillo, Texas, pediatrician who treated Kristen said in a deposition that he learned to use Botox on children with cerebral palsy at Allergan-sponsored seminars in 2000 and 2001.

Rolf Habersang, who is a critical care pediatrician and medical professor at Texas Tech University, and his nurse practitioner wife Pia both testified that they believed Allergan arranged and paid for them to fly to an Irving, Texas, seminar. Allergan also sent Dr. Habersang to Little Rock, Ark., to train with a pediatric neurologist, the Habersangs said.

The doctor testified that he learned to dose children with 15 units of Botox per kilogram of body weight.

That is nearly twice the maximum dosage that Allergan considers safe for children, according to the deposition testimony of Allergan executive and neurologist Mitchell Brin.

But, Brin testified, the company never shared its maximum dosage information with physicians because of a federal ban on marketing for non-approved uses that it believed prohibited such communications.

Still, Allergan's sales agents discussed the use of Botox for juvenile cerebral palsy patients with the Habersangs repeatedly, visiting the practice about 50 times over several years, according to motions and depositions. One sales agent told the Habersangs that other physicians were using Botox "in the range of 10 to 15" units per kilogram, Pia Habersang said in her deposition.

Allergan said in a court motion that Rolf Habersang was aware of the risks of Botox when he treated Kristen, although Habersang testified he was unaware of the reports of seizures and breathing, swallowing and other difficulties among pediatric cerebral palsy patients. He said he would have shared such information with parents.

In June 2006, the suit alleges Kristen's health was stable. Over the next 15 months, the 33-pound girl got seven Botox treatments in her legs, groin and chest.

Kristen's health deteriorated dramatically, the suit alleges. Already subject to seizures, Kristen got them more frequently, and they got worse, according to one motion. She was hospitalized 10 times for repeated bouts of breathing and swallowing difficulties and pneumonia, it says. About six weeks after her last treatment, Kristen stopped breathing.

She died on Nov. 24, 2007, at the age of 7.

[Editor's note: Spears lost her lawsuit against Allergan.]

Using Botox to Treat Cerebral Palsy Is Worth the Risk

Ellen Seidman

In the following viewpoint Ellen Seidman maintains that despite the risks of Botox, she will continue to get the injections for her son to treat his cerebral palsy. According to Seidman, there are few options available to treat the muscle tightness that plagues people with cerebral palsy. Of these options, Botox has provided her son with the most benefit in the shortest amount of time. Seidman sympathizes with the woman who is suing Botox-maker Allergan, alleging the drug caused her daughter's death; however, Seidman asserts that she is not going to stop giving her son treatment that has enhanced the quality of his life. Seidman is a writer and editor for the *Huffington Post*, an online daily newspaper.

I had two reactions to the news about the little girl with cerebral palsy [CP] who allegedly died as a result of getting Botox in her legs to prevent her muscles from having spasms:

SOURCE: Ellen Seidman, "A Child Dies from Getting Botox, a Mother Sues" originally appeared in *The Huffington Post*, February 3, 2010. Revised and updated July 2010. Reproduced by permission of the author. http://lovethatmax.blogspot.com.

- Uh-oh, it's been awhile since Max (my little boy) got a Botox injection, gotta get on the phone.
- Uh-oh, maybe I better not get him that Botox injection.

I'd venture that this is a typical mixed reaction you might get from a parent of a kid with special needs. It's hard not to be tempted by alternate treatments when mainstream medicine offers so few options. It's hard not to do whatever you possibly could to help your child and improve his or her quality of life.

Max also has cerebral palsy. He had a stroke at birth that caused brain damage. Max is seven, the same age as poor Kristen Spears of Potter County in Texas. Her mother is suing Botox manufacturer Allergan and claiming an overdose caused her daughter's death in 2007; the company is pointing to a bacterial infection unrelated to Botox. Like Kristen, Max has gotten Botox injections to help with muscle issues— in his case, tightness in his hands that made it hard for him to open them. It's an "off-label" usage of the drug—the company never licensed the drug to help muscle tightness in kids with cerebral palsy, though it's become common practice. Insurance paid for our treatments.

FAST FACT

According to the National Institute of Neurological Disorders and Stroke, the majority of individuals with cerebral palsy experience some form of premature aging by the time they reach their forties because of the extra stress and strain placed on their bodies.

Stem Cell Therapy

Over the years, my husband and I have always had the motto that if it couldn't hurt Max but it might help, we'd be willing to give it a go. It's why we've tried experimental treatments such as hyperbaric oxygen therapy in which you and your child (or your child alone) hang out in a tent or long glass infused with pure oxygen, which may help "awaken" dormant areas of the brain. My husband used to lie down in the tube with baby Max, and we'd joke that he was going to be the smartest dad in the whole wide world.

This past summer [of 2009], we got Max stem cell therapy at Duke University, using his cord blood that we'd banked at birth. The doctor doing the transplant, Dr. Joanne Kurtzberg, explained how stem cells work this way: "We believe that stem cells can travel to the brain and then help repair damage caused by stroke, low oxygen or other vascular problems. The cells may work in two ways, first by releasing hormones that calm down inflammation and also attract cells from the brain to heal damaged areas, and second, by providing stem cells to contribute to the repair."

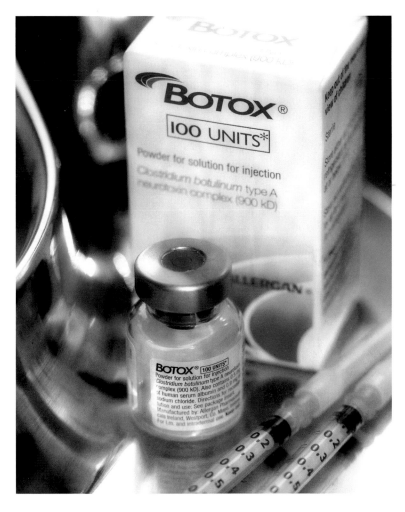

Allergan Corporation's Botox has been found effective in treating the muscle tightness that plagues people with cerebral palsy, although use of the drug is controversial. **(Saturn Stills/Photo Researchers, Inc.)**

Botox Works Fastest and Best

When you have a kid with special needs, as a parent you are so eager to do whatever you can to help your child. With cerebral palsy in particular, there aren't a whole lot of options for resolving muscle tightness. Physical therapy, massage, special splints and exercise can help, but for us (and other kids I know with CP), Botox has always been the thing that's provided the fastest and most apparent benefit. Botox has left Max's hands looser, and after getting the injections he's been better able to grasp objects and generally use his hands. Both his therapists and doctors have recommended the Botox injections; the physiatrist who did this procedure at the hospital (you go there and stay for several hours) does dozens of injections a month. I used to joke with friends about opening a mommy-child Botox clinic: Moms get a little Botox around the eyes to get rid of wrinkles, kids get Botox to relieve the stiffness.

Obviously, the Botox injections have taken a serious turn with the allegations that Botox led to this child's death. After getting injected, Kristen Spears had trouble with breathing and swallowing; it remains to be seen whether or not Botox played a role. [Spears lost her case in 2010.] As one doctor explained it, "All drugs have potential side effects and one side effect of Botox is that it can, on occasion, migrate from the injection site, to other muscle groups. When this hits the respiratory muscles, it can make breathing difficult."

Will Continue Son's Botox Treatments

I'm keeping an eye on this case. And before I schedule the next Botox appointment, I'm having a long conversation with the doctor. But will it stop me from getting my son Botox injections? I don't think so. This may no longer 100 percent fit the bill of "can't hurt" but at the same time, I can't just slam the door shut on something that has made it possible for Max to be able to better function and live his life.

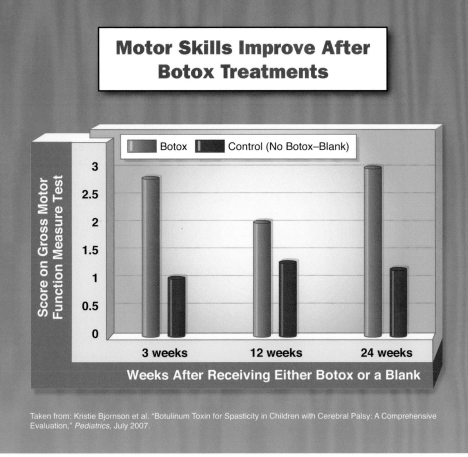

Motor Skills Improve After Botox Treatments

Score on Gross Motor Function Measure Test

Botox   Control (No Botox–Blank)

3
2.5
2
1.5
1
0.5
0

3 weeks   12 weeks   24 weeks

Weeks After Receiving Either Botox or a Blank

Taken from: Kristie Bjornson et al. "Botulinum Toxin for Spasticity in Children with Cerebral Palsy: A Comprehensive Evaluation," *Pediatrics*, July 2007.

It's a tough line you walk as the parent of a kid with special needs, making these major decisions for a child you so desperately want to help. This is yet another thing to add to my list of concerns. And, yeah, I may just need some Botox for those worry lines—but I won't be rushing to get it.

Complementary and Alternative Medicine May Help People with Cerebral Palsy

Gregory S. Liptak

In the following viewpoint Gregory S. Liptak asserts that complementary and alternative treatments for cerebral palsy are becoming increasingly popular and that doctors should acknowledge and discuss these treatment options with their patients. Liptak reviews the evidence behind several alternative therapies used by people with cerebral palsy, including hyperbaric oxygen treatment and the Adeli suit. He determines that while some alternative treatments seem to be beneficial for those with cerebral palsy, others warrant more research. Despite the absence of supporting evidence for some alternative therapies, Liptak contends that doctors owe it to their cerebral palsy patients to discuss all possible treatment options. Liptak is a pediatrics professor at the Upstate Medical Center of the State University of New York in Syracuse.

Cerebral Palsy (CP) is not a single condition, but rather is a group of disorders. It affects the brain and leads to problems with the ability to move

SOURCE: Gregory S. Liptak, "Complementary and Alternative Therapies for Cerebral Palsy," *Focus on Cerebral Palsy Newsletter,* March 2007. Reproduced by permission of the author.

and with other areas of development. CP is chronic and has no cure. Several newer treatments have been used to try to improve the functioning of children who have CP. These include treatments to decrease spasticity such as injections with Botox, surgery to place a Baclofen pump and surgery to cut certain nerve roots, called Selective Dorsal Rhizotomy.

Complementary and Alternative Medicine (CAM) has been defined as "a group of diverse medical and health care systems, practices, and products that are not presently considered to be part of conventional medicine." CAM includes 1) alternative medical systems such as traditional oriental medicine and naturopathy; 2) mind-body interventions, such as prayer healing and art therapy; 3) biological-based therapies such as herbal treatments and special diets; 4) manipulative and body-based methods, such as massage therapy and chiropractic manipulations; and 5) energy therapies such as electromagnetic-field therapy.

CAM is being promoted more often than ever before for children who have CP. In a recent survey, 56% of children and youth who had CP used one or more CAM techniques. Massage therapy (25%), aquatherapy (25%), and hippotherapy (equine-assisted therapy or horseback riding) (18%) were the most commonly used techniques. This article will review several of the more common complementary therapies and discuss the evidence that has been published on their effectiveness.

Equine-Assisted Therapy

Therapeutic horseback riding has been used with children who have disabilities since the 1950s when it was used primarily for children who had polio. Recently, it has become increasingly popular to use with children who have CP. Theoretically, riding on a horse can improve posture, balance, and overall function by mobilizing the pelvis, lumbar spine, and hip joints, decreasing muscle tone, improving head and trunk postural control, and developing equilibrium reactions in the trunk.

A number of studies without comparison groups have shown beneficial effects from horseback riding in children with CP. Improvements have been noted in walking, running, and jumping. In one study, the improvements lasted at least 16 weeks after the horseback riding was stopped. In one controlled trial, children with spastic Cerebral Palsy were randomized to eight minutes of Hippotherapy or eight minutes sitting astride a stationary barrel. They found significant improvement in muscle groups that had the most asymmetry prior to Hippotherapy. No significant change was noted after sitting astride a barrel.

Equine-assisted therapy, or hippotherapy, has long been an effective therapeutic treatment for people with disabilities, but only recently has it been used with success in the treatment of cerebral palsy. **(Huy Richard Mach/MCT/Landov)**

Thus, both uncontrolled and controlled trials have shown benefits from Hippotherapy. In addition, riding on a horse is fun and increases the social participation of the child with CP. Other activities like adapted skiing and hydrotherapy have not been studied as extensively as horseback riding, but similarly would be engaging, enjoyable and increase participation in recreational activities.

Acupuncture

Acupuncture is based on a complex theory. According to traditional Chinese medicine, health is achieved by maintaining an uninterrupted flow of Qi, or energy, along 14 meridians. Disease is caused by stagnation of the flow of Qi, and by an imbalance between yin and yang. Acupuncture can help reestablish the normal flow of Qi, thus restoring internal balance and health. In acupuncture, fine needles are inserted into precisely defined, specific points on the body to correct disruptions in harmony. Electrical current may be applied through the needles. Sessions typically last for 15 to 20 minutes and are administered several times a week.

Acupuncture has been used to treat children with Cerebral Palsy for more than 20 years. Most studies published in English, however, have been recent and uncontrolled. Benefits attributed to acupuncture for children with CP include warmer hands and feet, decrease in painful spasms, improvement in the use of arms or legs, more restful sleep, improvements in mood, and improved bowel function.

In a controlled trial, acupuncture was applied to the tongue over 30 sessions. Children receiving the therapy had significant improvements in drooling. In another study of acupuncture applied to the tongue, children in the group receiving treatment had better gross motor scores. Thus, uncontrolled studies have shown improvements in several areas; two controlled trials also showed improvements.

Adeli Suit

The Adeli Suit originally was developed for Russian cosmonauts to counteract the effects of zero gravity, including muscle atrophy and osteopenia (thinning of bones). The suit had rings placed on it to allow elastic cords to be attached across joints. The suit, as modified for children, consists of a vest, shorts, headpiece, and knee pads. A wide belt with rings is worn at the hips. The belt is connected to shoes and kneepads, and a head piece can be provided for patients with poor head control. It allows controlled exercise against resistance, similar to the use of weights as well as changes to posture. For example, if a child has lordosis [a swayback or saddleback], cords can be placed to increase extension of the hips and flexion of the lower abdomen. The suit works as an elastic frame surrounding the body, with the elastic cords creating tension, theoretically developing the muscles in the legs and arms. . . .

Treatments are administered from ½ to 2 hours a day, five to six days a week for four weeks under the direct supervision of a physical therapist. Other types of therapy, including stretching and functional activities are included as part of the intervention.

No published evidence from a controlled trial is available in English to support or reject the use of the suit. Thus, no conclusive evidence either in support of or against the use of the Adeli suit is available. Based on two unpublished studies, the United Cerebral Palsy Association concluded, "These studies show that a period of intensive therapy in ambulatory children with cerebral palsy can lead to improvement in a number of disabilities. However, they did not demonstrate that use of the Adeli Suit was helpful. Any effect is likely to be minor." . . .

Hyperbaric Oxygen Treatment

Hyperbaric Oxygen Treatment (HBOT) is the delivery of 100% oxygen under pressure. Its advocates have argued that "dormant areas" can be found surrounding injured areas in the brains of children with CP. High levels of oxygen in the brain reactivate, or "wake up" the cells of this dormant area. Some have argued that the oxygen can induce DNA to stimulate cell repair. It is also believed that hyperbaric oxygen therapy reduces swelling in the brain by constricting blood vessels, and "provides an ideal internal environment for the growth of new brain tissue." Pressures of 1.5 to 1.75 Atmospheres (the equivalent of 25 feet below sea level) typically are used. Each treatment lasts one hour and one or two treatments are prescribed each day, five or six days per week. It is common to administer 40 treatments in the first phase of treatment. Potential bad effects include problems with the ear, including pain, perforation and bleeding, pneumothorax (rupture of the sacs in the lung), myopia, fire or explosions, and oxygen-induced convulsions.

In an uncontrolled study, 25 children with CP received 20 treatments at 1.75 atmospheres for 60 minutes each. They showed improved gross motor and fine motor

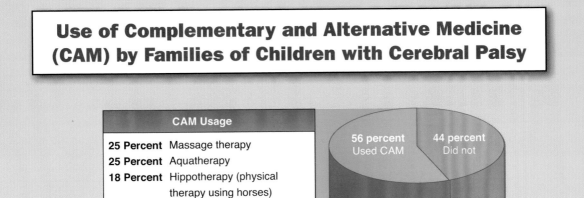

Use of Complementary and Alternative Medicine (CAM) by Families of Children with Cerebral Palsy

CAM Usage	
25 Percent	Massage therapy
25 Percent	Aquatherapy
18 Percent	Hippotherapy (physical therapy using horses)
12 Percent	Chiropractic
6 Percent	Adeli suit
6 Percent	Hyperbaric oxygen therapy

*Figures are approximate, due to rounding

56 percent Used CAM — 44 percent Did not

Taken from: Edward A. Hurvitz et al. "Complementary and Alternative Medicine Use in Families of Children with Cerebral Palsy," *Developmental Medicine and Child Neurology*, 2003.

functioning and reduced spasticity. In an unpublished study, children with CP were randomized to immediate therapy with hyperbaric oxygen or a six month delay in treatment. Improvements in parental reports of attention, language and play were reported. However, no objective differences were noted by observers who viewed videotapes and were blinded to group membership.

A blinded, randomized, controlled clinical trial of 111 children was conducted in Quebec. The children in the treatment group received 40 treatments of hyperbaric oxygen at 1.75 atmospheres, while the children in the control group received air at a pressure of 1.3 atmospheres. Interestingly, both groups showed significant improvements in gross motor abilities, cognition, communication, and memory. However, no additional benefits were found from the oxygen. In this study, 27 of the 49 children (55%) in the hyperbaric oxygen group and 15 of the 52 children (29%) in the slightly pressurized air group had ear problems. Some have argued that these findings demonstrate the value of elevated oxygen, even at minimal levels. Others have argued that it demonstrates a "powerful clinical trials effect," i.e., highly motivated parents spent many hours with their children in an intensive setting, knowing that developmental outcomes would be evaluated.

A formal evaluation of published research on the use of hyperbaric oxygen commissioned by the Agency for Healthcare Research and Quality concluded that, "There is insufficient evidence to determine whether the use of HBOT improves functional outcomes in children with cerebral palsy." . . .

The individual with Cerebral Palsy and his or her family have a right to full disclosure of all possible treatment options. The best practice of medicine combines the art (individual clinical expertise) with the science (clini-

> **FAST FACT**
>
> According to the National Center for Health Statistics, about 12 percent of children in the United States used complementary and alternative medicine in 2007.

cal evidence from systematic research). The care of patients should be based, to the greatest extent possible, on evidence, whether or not the therapy is considered to be complementary. This means that sound evidence exists that (1) the therapy recommended is effective in reducing suffering or improving function; (2) the benefits outweigh the risks; (3) the cost of the treatment is reasonable compared to its expected benefits; and (4) the recommended therapy is practical, acceptable, and feasible.

CHAPTER 3

Personal Experiences with Cerebral Palsy

Facing Fears and Climbing Mountains

Bonner Paddock, Interviewed by Brian Helfrich

In the following selection Brian Helfrich interviews Bonner Paddock, an executive with the National Hockey League team the Anaheim Mighty Ducks. The interview took place while Paddock, who has cerebral palsy, was preparing to climb Mount Kilimanjaro, which at fifteen thousand feet is the tallest mountain in Africa. Paddock talks to Helfrich about how cerebral palsy has affected his life and what motivates him to climb to the top of the mountain. Helfrich is a writer for the magazine *Sports Business Daily*.

I n the last two years, [Anaheim Mighty] Ducks Senior Manager of Corporate Partnerships Bonner Paddock has run a marathon and climbed a mountain, which is a bundle to handle for any exec, especially one battling cerebral palsy [CP]. Inspired by a philanthropic effort by Ducks co-owners Henry and Susan Samueli in '05, Paddock has

SOURCE: Brian Helfrich, "Interview: Catching Up With Bonnor Paddock Before He Summits Kilamanjaro," *Sports Business Daily*, August 1, 2008. Copyright © 2008 Street & Smith's Sports Group and its licensors. All rights reserved. Reproduced by permission.

Photo on facing page.
A teaching assistant helps a girl with cerebral palsy use an alternative communication device during a speech class. Children with cerebral palsy need special education and care as part of their daily lives.
(Ellen B. Senisi/Photo Researchers, Inc.)

tackled his disability head on, and next month [September 2008] will travel to Tanzania and attempt to summit Mt. Kilimanjaro as part of a fundraising effort. . . . Paddock last year [2007] was awarded the Life Without Limits Award from United Cerebral Palsy of Orange County, and his trip to Africa will be captured for an upcoming documentary. Before tackling his newest adventure, Paddock took time to talk with Staff Writer Brian Helfrich. . . .

Facing Fears

Helfrich: You just climbed Mt. Whitney and last year ran a marathon, but where did the idea for Mt. Kilimanjaro come from?

Paddock: For most of my life, my family never talked about my disability because I was doing well, and the doctors said, "If he's not doing badly, let's not make him that aware of it. You don't want to get it in his head that he can't do things." When I got to the Ducks, we were in the middle of the lockout and the Samuelis had just signed the purchase letter, so we didn't have as much to do at the time. The Samuelis said, "I know we're going to be the new owners and we just want to encourage everybody during this time to join a charity that you feel passionate about." So I started talking to my mom a little bit more about cerebral palsy, learned more about it and started volunteering. It's one of those things that I started facing all my fears, which had anything to do with my balance or my lower body. Then I ran the marathon, and had people, including [Ducks executive vice president and general manager] Brian Burke and his wife, supporting me, and it made me realize it was OK to face these fears. And Kilimanjaro has every fear in my life. I don't have equilibrium so I have to balance with my eyes. We start the final summit night at around 2:00 am in the thin air, so I'm real nervous about my balance. But I'm just trying to face all my fears and hopefully show all these other kids who have disabilities and may be afraid to do something that it's OK to give it a try, and if you put your mind to it, you can do it. And hopefully that's what I can prove.

Could you talk about what physical shortcomings as a result of CP make it so challenging for you to climb a mountain?

My biggest struggles are my balance and lower body. The parts of my brain that were damaged or non-functional at birth were my equilibrium and lower body strength and coordination. I balance with my eyes. I use walls, poles, etc. to set my parameters and relative body position. When I get tired, my balance is the first thing that I really struggle with. When I am tired it is harder to concentrate on things and focus on body position. My walk has a limp. A lot of people ask if I have a bad knee, hip or ankle. I was able to play sports but the ones with footwork were harder for me. I loved to play as many sports as I could. Wasn't always the best athlete, but had a ton of determination and hated to fail at anything. I wear my shoes out severely on the insides and the toes of the shoes. Dress shoes don't last long for me. I spent countless years going to physical therapy five days a week. It helped me tremendously because I had extremely tight hamstrings, etc. It made my toes grip inward when I was younger until we started physical therapy.

> **FAST FACT**
>
> According to the National Institute of Neurological Disorders and Stroke, the incidence of depression is three to four times higher in people with disabilities such as cerebral palsy.

Have you considered what you may want to tackle after Kilimanjaro?

I don't know, because it took almost a year for my body to recover from the marathon, and I'm not doing so well the day after summiting Mt. Whitney. It was a good idea and it was not such a good idea. I wanted to see if my body would shut down, and I really had some bad problems on the way down. I had severe cramping in my stomach and lower body. Obviously my feet are really messed up because [of] the way I walk, but I wasn't anticipating it being that bad. The boots are heavy. But I did make the summit on Saturday [July 26, 2008]. After starting at 3:30 am, we summited at 11:55 am and arrived back down at the bottom at 6:30 pm. It was the hardest thing I have ever done. But going forward, I know I could do more, so I definitely anticipate coming up with something. I know I couldn't do Everest. But Kilimanjaro just came up as a way to face my fears. Maybe after I get back I will sit down and figure out what else I fear. I have to continue doing stuff in my life, because I've been given something 99% of these other kids haven't.

Aside from raising money, what else do you hope to gain from the Kilimanjaro trip?

Most of it already happened, and it's some stuff that I didn't even expect. A friend of a friend met me at a game and ends up selling his bike for $50. Fifty bucks for an 11-year-old kid is like thousands of dollars. It was unbelievable. And a girl set up a lemonade stand and made $600 in two hours. She was the most remarkable, because she has a more severe case of CP than I do. Her family read the front-page story written in the *Orange County Register* and contacted me through that. They wanted her to meet me, and then she went home that night and thinks of the lemonade stand on her own. All of her friends have opened lemonade stands on the weekends and have raised $1,500—just 11-year-old girls putting up lemonade stands on street corners.

What would you say was more exciting—the Ducks winning the Stanley Cup [hockey championship] or you winning the Life Without Limits Award?

(Laughs). Both were unexpected. I never took the job at the Ducks thinking they were going to win a championship, especially where they were before the lockout. So that was a huge surprise. The Life Without Limits Award was tough, because I'm still struggling and working on talking about having a disability. They were both emotional, one for one reason, and one for the other. One is a personal satisfaction, while the other is more of a business satisfaction.

You mention Burke and getting the inspiration from the Samuelis. How supportive have the Ducks been throughout all your endeavors?

They've been huge supporters. They've definitely jumped behind all of this, and I just got an e-mail from the NHL today saying that they wanted to do something with their Web site. It's really cool that the league is not only acknowledging what the players are doing, but front-office people who are trying to make a difference too. . . .

Who else have you talked to about getting involved?

I don't know if they'll do anything, but we are talking to ESPN's "Outside the Lines." The woman I hired to help me, because I realized I got way in over my head, she was reaching out to them. And I'm in touch with [actor] Colin Farrell's people about narrating the documentary, and those talks have been very positive because his son has the same disability as I do.

You read a quote every day. Are there any that have stuck with you?

Two. Vince Lombardi said, "If you believe in yourself and have the courage, the determination, the dedication, the competitive drive and if you are willing to sacrifice the little things in life and pay the price for the things that are worthwhile, it can be done." And Lance Armstrong said, "Pain is temporary, it may last a minute, or an hour, or a year, but eventually it will subside and something else will take its place. If I quit, however, it lasts forever." That was the one I kept thinking about while I was going up Mt. Whitney.

Focusing on Ability, Not Disability

Glenda Watson Hyatt, Interviewed by Fernanda

In the following selection a young woman with cerebral palsy, Glenda Watson Hyatt, is interviewed by a student named Fernanda, who is the master's degree program in applied disability studies at Brock University in Ontario, Canada. Hyatt's cerebral palsy has left her functionally nonverbal and dependent on a wheelchair for mobility. Fernanda asks Hyatt questions about how she feels about her disability, how others have treated her because of her disability, and whether she is angry or feels sorry for herself. Glenda reveals strength and courage, asserting that there is no reason for self-pity. Hyatt can only use her left thumb to type, but she writes a blog and has authored a book. She hopes that by sharing her story she will inspire and motivate others who struggle with disabilities. Hyatt is married and lives in Canada where she writes and works to improve the accessibility of Web sites for people with disabilities.

SOURCE: Fernanda, "Interview: Life with Cerebral Palsy: A Masters in Applied Disabilities Studies with Glenda Watson Hyatt," *Doitmyselfblog.com*, November 19, 2008. Reproduced by permission.

Saturday [November 15, 2008] I received an interview request from Fernanda for an assignment for her Masters degree in Applied Disability Studies at Brock University. I concurred. I asked if I could share the interview with my blog readers. She concurred.

Fernanda: How was your parents' reaction when they found out that their baby had Cerebral Palsy [CP]?

Glenda Watson Hyatt: Initially, they were understandably shocked with the complications of my birth and the following few days. Then they were fairly matter-of-fact; this is the situation, what do we do to make the most of it? The official diagnosis came later. By then, they knew I had some kind of disability. Mom might have even known it was CP. The diagnosis gave them confirmation and a label that Mom then began researching at the medical library at the University of British Columbia where she was a student—she was in Education, getting her specialty in Special Education.

How was the support from the rest of your family?

My family has always been very supportive. I'm not sure my Grandma (my Dad's mom) fully understood, but she did accept me in her own way.

Did your parents have any kind of difficulty to register you in a regular school?

I began my schooling in a special education class and was gradually integrated into a regular class. Beginning in Grade Eight, I attended our local high school. Near the end of Grade Seven, I went through some testing with the school psychologist, which I didn't think was fair since my fellow classmates didn't have to go through the same testing. The results were to convince the high school staff that I was capable of handling the regular curriculum. Once I began Grade Eight and had proven what I was capable of, their concerns dissipated. Being on the Honour Roll my first semester clinched it.

Did you have any problem to be accepted in your school and/or in your community?

For the most part, I didn't have a problem with other kids teasing me in high school. When I started in Brownies back in elementary school, the girls fought over who would push my small red wheelchair. They saw it as a special privilege. A few friendships from high school and Brownies/Girl Guides still exist today. Those ones are dear to me.

No Self-Pity

Did you ever ask why me?

No, not really; at least not for any length of time. I see my cerebral palsy as something that is. No amount of crying and self-pity is going to change that fact. I might as well get on with it and make the most of what I do have. There is so much I can do; I try to focus on that.

In your daily life, you face challenges all the time. Simple things that we take for granted like opening the door, turning the lights off and other rather mundane tasks constitute a challenge for you. Where do you find strength to fight and don't get bitter?

Yes, simple things can be frustrating, even extremely frustrating at times. I keep trying until I get it or find a way around it. Otherwise, I would be sitting in the dark!

In the really tough moments, I think about my Nanna (my Mom's mom). She had bone cancer. She crawled up and down the old wood stairs to do the laundry in the basement. I figure if she could do that, then I [can] deal with my minute frustration or pain in the moment.

Can you tell me if you had any kind of situation in your life that made you feel really angry and/or upset with society?

Searching for a job was tough. All of my life, I had been told to try my best and to work hard, and that I could do anything I wanted. My disability didn't matter. But when I went for interviews, it felt like the employ-

> **FAST FACT**
>
> According to the National Institute of Neurological Disorders and Stroke, about 20 percent of children with cerebral palsy are unable to produce intelligible speech.

ers couldn't see beyond my disability to see my abilities, skills and talents. They didn't give me the opportunity to try and to prove what I could do. That really hurt and was very discouraging.

What do you think that politicians and big companies should do to help people with disabilities feel included in our society?

There is so much they could do to include people with disabilities in society. Briefly, two main areas are:

- accessibility, in every possible way—from infrastructure (buildings, transportation and community planning) to health care, to web accessibility, to access to services, to product development, to the electoral process and the list goes on; and
- meaningful job creation and employment, with adequate supports and opportunities for further training and career advancement.

When did you have the idea to write your autobiography?

When I was ten, I read books like *Joni, Other Side of the Mountain* and *Ice Castles*, which [are] about people with disabilities; actually, young women with disabilities. At that time, they were my only role models with disabilities. I decided that one day I would share my life to help others in a similar way. Thirty years later I self-published *I'll Do It Myself.*

What makes you feel free?

Driving in my scooter with the sun and a big smile on my face—and plenty of accessible sidewalk!

A Teen Triumphs over His Disability

Keith

In the following selection a teenager named Keith talks about growing up with cerebral palsy. Keith says the leg braces he had to wear
in high school to maintain range of motion made him a target for
bullies and insensitive people. But Keith learned how to respond to
these people by learning to laugh at himself. Finding the humor in
life and staying positive has enabled Keith to excel in sports and
marching band and to ask girls out on dates. Keith believes having
cerebral palsy has taught him to never give up and has contributed to his success as a person. Keith's story is featured on the
Nemours Pediatric Health Systems' TeensHealth Web site.

Apparently, having cerebral palsy makes me different.

I've had cerebral palsy since birth and I'll have
it until I'm old and grey. There isn't a day that I'm not
reminded I have the condition. And there never will be
a day I won't have it. But in my mind's eye, life is good:

SOURCE: Keith, "Cerebral Palsy: Keith's Story," Teenshealth.org,
April 2009. Copyright © 1995–2010 The Nemours Foundation. All
rights reserved. Reproduced by permission.

If anything, cerebral palsy has made me a stronger, more humble person. I can even say having cerebral palsy has contributed to my success.

Cerebral palsy—CP for short—is a condition caused by injury to the parts of the brain that control our ability to use our muscles and bodies. *Cerebral* means having to do with the brain. *Palsy* means weakness or problems with using the muscles. Often the injury happens before birth. Sometimes it happens when a baby is being delivered or soon after being born. CP can be mild, moderate, or severe.

I'm in college now. As a teen with CP it was easy for me to get overlooked, discouraged, or even patronized simply because I wasn't considered "normal." This became especially apparent when doctors began prescribing "special devices" to help me re-establish or maintain a "suitable range of motion." These devices were to be worn while doing everyday activities, *including* school-time activities.

Because my CP mostly affects my legs and the way I walk, I had to wear knee-high, white-plastic, custom-made leg braces at all times during my first couple of years of high school.

Laced with Velcro, these braces locked my ankles and heel cords in a fixed position. Needless to say I hated those braces! They were painful, noisy—thanks to the Velcro and cheap plastic—and they seemed to broadcast that I was "crippled" (my skin crawls when I hear that word).

Fortunately, I have a very mild case of CP, and only my walk is affected. My hamstrings and heel cords are spastic (meaning they might twitch or spasm on their own and I can't control them) or tight. This causes me to walk bent-kneed and on my toes.

For people with more severe cases of CP, all aspects of their physical abilities—and sometimes even mental abilities—can be limited. I was fortunate that my legs were only slightly affected, which allowed me to participate in gym, school sports, and marching band. I was even bold enough to take part in school productions and plays.

I'm Rubber and Bullies Are Glue

As mild as my case of CP may be, there were always the high school bullies who found pleasure in bringing me down. Sometimes it felt that the only reason they were in school that day was to be my rain cloud, following me around, pointing out my mistakes and flaws.

My bullies were girls as well as guys. They weren't physically threatening. They were the kind who hurt with words or by forcing an embarrassing situation, constantly looking over a shoulder for supporting chuckles from friends. However, my bullies normally found themselves laughing alone, because I'd already beaten them to the punchline. I was well liked, so the joke was on them. The reality was they had a lot of catching up to do.

A bully can't compare to what you put yourself through mentally. Just entertaining the thought that you're not the same as everyone else can work against anyone, even when you know you're above the norm in so many ways. During school, I never wasted time worrying what other people thought of me. I mostly worked on staying positive and meeting my own standards and expectations.

But there were times when people really got to me—their harassing, hurtful words began to penetrate. A couple of times, I even caught myself thinking, "What if they're right?" I found this the hardest place mentally to pull myself out of. But I told myself what I knew to be true: "*You're the one who's right!* It doesn't matter what *they* think, you know you're better than them simply because you don't resort to acting like them. They are making you feel like an outcast so that their pitiful lives don't look so worthless after all."

As a teen, most of our time is spent in school. I found it doesn't do any good to avoid the people who put me in these mental dark places. Instead, I worked on beating them to the punchline, turning the joke on them. This helped me develop a great life skill: the art of the witty comeback.

Dating for Dreamers

Having CP and dealing with bullies is a breeze compared with dealing with the anxiety of asking your first crush out on a date!

To me—and lots of guys!—high school girls seemed unpredictable and hard to figure out. The only thing I could do was be likeable, engaging, and responsive. The hardest obstacle to overcome was starting the first conversation. A lot of guys think they don't have anything interesting to talk about. This is where having CP came in handy!

When I was in ninth grade, there was a girl I liked who happened to be in all my classes. Soon, I got noticed and curiosity got the best of her. She was forced to ask the question that was on her mind for some time, "What's wrong with your legs?" These weren't the most romantic words to start a relationship, but it got my "foot in the door."

When most guys are struggling for the attention of the girls they like (by making fun of people like me!), I have the advantage because people are naturally curious, and all I have to do is smile. I was responsive to the girl I liked, so it made it easier for her to talk to me, even if the ice-breaking question was a bit embarrassing.

Don't count yourself out when it comes to dating. People will like you for who you are—that's it!

Spastic About Sports

The same theme of having a positive attitude and a willingness to try can be applied to cerebral palsy and sports. I played many sports while I was in high school, but I was best at golf. Go figure: the one sport that requires balance and precision—two weapons that aren't readily available in my arsenal. But I really excelled at golf.

My doctor explained how I was able to participate—and achieve—as well as I did in sports, particularly golf: It's possible for some people with CP to learn how to get our bodies to work in other ways. In my case, I figured out how to use different back, arm, and leg muscles to mimic the techniques of the golf swing, instinctively adapting to my body's limitations.

I would have never known that my body was able to adapt like this if I didn't have the courage to try to play. I knew that I might fail, but I also knew that there was a greater possibility I'd have fun. I wasn't afraid what the other members of the team would think of me, because by this time my reputation and positive mindset preceded me. I say this because I want to stress the importance of staying positive about CP—or any physical condition— and not think of it as a limitation.

In my experience, people tend to admire you most for trying. They want to see you succeed, sometimes more than succeeding themselves. Four years of varsity golf was one of the highlights of my high school career and some of my best friends in school played golf.

I also participated in wrestling, working up to competing on the varsity level as well. Although I wasn't the best, I kept with it and tried my hardest. My body adapted its own techniques, like in golf.

In my case, participating in as many physical activities as possible was the best way (other than physical therapy or occupational therapy) to combat CP. Exercise keeps the affected muscles loose and limber, which helps to counteract the appearance of cerebral palsy.

Marching to the Beat of a Different Drummer

"Life is not about fitting in; it's about standing out." I don't know who originally said that, but it became my mantra when I joined the marching band. That's right: Keith, the guy writing about walking funny, joined the marching band as a freshman in high school.

Why? I really enjoy playing instruments, and in my high school, if you wanted to be in any band, you had to join marching band. It was a requirement: If you didn't join marching band, you couldn't play at all.

That's how I found myself standing in the middle of a football field, trying out for the only high school sport where judges strictly critique the way you walk—no pressure there!

Being a member of a nationally recognized marching band is one of my more significant high school accomplishments. Although I can't say for sure how much harder it was for me than the rest of the band to keep step and pace while maintaining musical integrity, I can assure you that wrestling doesn't even come close to being as physically demanding.

Imagine standing on the 50-yard line of a football field as proud and as tall as physically possible while holding a 5-pound instrument up to your face. The conductor is counting 1-2-3-4-1-2; you're marching in time. Now put yourself in my position: Imagine doing this with a large rubber band wrapped around your knees—but still maintain your form, remember all your notes, project your sound high . . . left foot . . . right foot . . . backward, forward, sideways . . . LOUDER. You can't make any mistakes, because the judges see everything. I bet you can see why I stuck with it for 9 out of 12 months for all 4 years of high school!

> **FAST FACT**
>
> According to the Christopher and Dana Reeve Foundation, in 2008 there were 412,000 people in the United States living with some form of paralysis caused by cerebral palsy.

The message here is, don't get discouraged by your physical limitations. There is no physical way that my marching technique was anywhere close to being technically sound, but I tried my hardest, and I never gave up. Over the 4 years, my marching band and I won numerous regional and state level championships; in this case it wasn't so bad to "stand out."

Whether I'm winning or losing, young or old, I will always have CP. That will make me different from everyone else, but it is up to me to decide how differently I present myself. For me, CP is not an excuse for bitterness or negative actions, but more of a reason to better myself or an excuse to try harder and be more successful.

Life can be funny, so why not beat it to the punchline?

GLOSSARY

Adeli suit A modification of the Russian cosmonaut Penguin suit, designed so the wearer moves body parts against resistance, thus improving muscle strength.

anticholinergic drugs A family of drugs that inhibit parasympathetic neural activity by blocking the neurotransmitter acetylcholine, which energizes muscle tissue.

Apgar score A numbered scoring system doctors use to assess a baby's physical state at the time of birth.

asphyxia Lack of oxygen; in the case of cerebral palsy, lack of oxygen to the brain.

assistive technology Equipment used to increase, maintain, or improve the functional capabilities of individuals with disabilities.

ataxia A deficiency of muscular coordination, especially when voluntary movements are attempted, such as grasping or walking.

athetosis A condition marked by slow, writhing, involuntary muscle movements.

Baclofen A muscle relaxant and antispasmodic that decreases the excitability of nerve cells in the spinal cord and is used to diminish spasticity in the lower limbs in persons with cerebral palsy and other diseases.

Baclofen pump A pump implanted under the skin of the abdomen that is programmed to release desired amounts of Baclofen into the spinal fluid around the spinal cord.

Botox (botulinum toxin) A drug commonly used to relax spastic muscles; it blocks the release of acetylcholine, a neurotransmitter that energizes muscle tissue.

cerebral	Relating to the cerebrum, the two hemispheres of the human brain.
cerebral palsy	An umbrella term encompassing a group of nonprogressive, noncontagious motor conditions that cause physical disability in human development, chiefly in the areas of body movement.
computed tomography (CT) scan	An imaging technique that uses X-rays and a computer to create a picture of bodily tissues and structures.
congenital cerebral palsy	Cerebral palsy that is present at birth from causes that have occurred during fetal development.
contracture	A tightening of muscles that prevents normal movement of the associated limb or other body part.
developmental disability	A disability or impairment beginning in infancy or childhood that may be expected to continue indefinitely and that causes a substantial disability.
diplegia	Paralysis affecting like parts on both sides of the body, such as both arms or both legs.
dorsal rhizotomy	A surgical procedure that cuts nerve roots to reduce spasticity in affected muscles.
dyskinesia	Impaired ability to make voluntary movements.
hemiplegia	Paralysis of one side of the body.
hippotherapy	Therapeutic horseback riding in order to help normalize muscle tone, equilibrium reactions, head and trunk control, coordination and spatial orientation. It is proposed that the multidimensional swinging rhythm of the horse's walk is transferred to the patient's pelvis in a manner that duplicates the normal human gait.
hyperbaric oxygen therapy	Oxygen delivered under increased pressure. It is also the term used for a procedure in which a person is placed in an apparatus that delivers, under increased atmospheric pressure, additional oxygen to the lungs and its blood vessels or to a wound.
intracerebral hemorrhage	Bleeding in the brain.

intrapartum asphyxia	The reduction or total stoppage of oxygen circulating in a baby's brain during labor and delivery.
lordosis	A swayback caused by an increased inward curvature of the lower spine.
magnetic resonance imaging (MRI)	An imaging technique that uses radio waves, magnetic fields, and computer analysis to create a picture of body tissues and structures.
mental retardation	According to the American Association on Mental Retardation, mental retardation is a disability that occurs before age eighteen characterized by significant limitations in intellectual functioning and adaptive behavior as expressed in conceptual, social, and practical adaptive skills. It is diagnosed through the use of standardized tests of intelligence and adaptive behavior.
muscle tone	The amount of a muscle's contraction when it is at rest. When too high, it is called spasticity; when too low, hypotonia. Both interfere with movement.
neuronal migration	The process in the developing brain, which occurs as early as the second month of gestation, in which neurons migrate from where they originate to where they settle into neural circuits and which is controlled in the brain by chemical guides and signals.
neuroprotective	Describes substances that protect nerve cells from damage or death.
off-label drugs	Drugs prescribed to treat conditions other than those that have been approved by the Food and Drug Administration.
osteopenia	Reduced density and mass of the bones.
palsy	Paralysis, or the lack of control over voluntary movement.
periventricular leukomalacia (PVL)	*Peri* means "near, or around"; *ventricular* refers to the ventricles or fluid spaces of the brain; and *leukomalacia* (literally, "white softening") refers to a softening of the white matter of the brain. PVL is a condition in which the cells that make up the brain's white matter die near the ventricles.

physical therapy (PT)	A clinical program aimed at improving motor skills, particularly gross motor skills.
quadriplegia	Paralysis of all four limbs.
range of motion	The degree of movement present at a joint.
rigidity	Extremely high muscle tone in any position, combined with very limited movement.
scoliosis	A disease of the spine in which the spinal column tilts or curves to one side of the body.
serial casting	A series of casts designed to gradually move a limb into a more functional position.
spastic	A condition in which the muscles are rigid, posture may be abnormal, and fine motor control is impaired.
static encephalopathy	A disease of the brain that does not get better or worse.
tenotomy	A surgical procedure that cuts the tendon of a contracted muscle to allow lengthening of the muscle.
tremor	An involuntary trembling or quivering.

CHRONOLOGY

1861 An English orthopedic surgeon, William John Little, publishes a paper describing the neurological problems of children with spastic diplegia, a form of cerebral palsy. The disease is primarily known as "Little's Disease" or "Cerebral Paralysis." Little attributes the cause of the disorder to a lack of oxygen during the birth process.

1889 Sir William Osler publishes the book *The Cerebral Palsies of Children: A Clinical Study from the Infirmary for Nervous Diseases*, and popularizes the term *cerebral palsy.*

1897 Sigmund Freud suggests that cerebral palsy might be caused by abnormal brain development instead of by a complication of birth.

1920s The drug Baclofen, a muscle relaxant and antispasmodic developed for the treatment of epilepsy, is found to decrease spasticity.

1939 The first March of Dimes chapter is established in Coshocton, Ohio, to support research to prevent birth defects and to promote the health of babies.

1945 Clement Smith publishes *The Physiology of the Newborn Infant.*

1952 Virginia Apgar develops the Apgar Score, a clinical system for evaluating an infant's physical condition at birth.

1959   Bronson Crothers and Richmond S. Paine publish the classic reference book *The Natural History of Cerebral Palsy.* The comprehensive book is based on a study of some eighteen hundred individuals with cerebral palsy examined between 1930 and 1950.

1979   Eugene Bleck publishes the classic book *Orthopaedic Management in Cerebral Palsy.*

1980s   Scientists funded by the National Institute of Neurological Disorders and Stroke analyze data from more than thirty-five thousand newborns and their mothers and discover that complications during birth and labor account for only a fraction of the infants born with cerebral palsy—probably less than 10 percent.

1990   Congress enacts the Americans with Disabilities Act.

1991   The Food and Drug Administration approves Botox for the treatment of dynamic muscle contracture in pediatric cerebral palsy patients.

1997   American researchers Robert Palisano, Peter Rosenbaum, Stephen Walter, Dianne Russell, and Barbara Galuppi develop the Gross Motor Function Classification System, or GMFCS, a five-level system to classify the gross motor function of children with cerebral palsy.

1998   Congress passes the Birth Defects Prevention Act of 1998.

2009   The American College of Obstetricians and Gynecologists issues an updated practice bulletin on the use of continuous electronic fetal monitoring during labor.

ORGANIZATIONS TO CONTACT

The editors have compiled the following list of organizations concerned with the issues debated in this book. The descriptions are derived from materials provided by the organizations. All have publications or information available for interested readers. The list was compiled on the date of publication of the present volume; the information provided here may change. Be aware that many organizations take several weeks or longer to respond to inquiries, so allow as much time as possible.

American Academy for Cerebral Palsy and Developmental Medicine
555 E. Wells St., Ste. 1100, Milwaukee, WI 53202
(414) 918-3014
fax: (414) 276-2146
e-mail: info@aacpdm .org
Web site: www.aacpdm .org

The American Academy for Cerebral Palsy and Developmental Medicine is a member organization that seeks to provide multidisciplinary scientific education for health professionals and promote excellence in research and services for the benefit of people with cerebral palsy and childhood-onset disabilities. The organization publishes the journal *Developmental Medicine & Child Neurology* as well as a monthly newsletter.

American College of Obstetricians and Gynecologists (ACOG)
409 Twelfth St. SW
PO Box 96920, Washington, DC 20090-6920
(202) 638-5577
Web site: www.acog.org

ACOG is a nonprofit organization of professionals providing health care for women. ACOG advocates for quality health care for women, promotes patient education, and increases awareness among its members and the public of the changing issues facing women's health care. ACOG issues relevant guidelines and bulletins and publishes several journals, including *Obstetrics & Gynecology* and *Special Issues in Women's Health*.

Birth Defect Research for Children, Inc. (BDRC)
800 Celebration Ave. Ste. 225, Celebration, FL 34747
(407) 566-8304
fax: (407) 566-8341
Web site: www.birth defects.org

The BDRC is a nonprofit organization that provides parents and expectant parents with information about birth defects and support services for their children. The BDRC has a parent-matching program that links families who have children with similar birth defects. The BDRC also sponsors the National Birth Defect Registry, a research project that studies associations between birth defects and exposures to radiation, medication, alcohol, smoking, chemicals, pesticides, lead, mercury, dioxin, and other environmental toxins.

Centers for Disease Control and Prevention (CDC) National Center on Birth Defects and Developmental Disabilities (NCBDDD)
1600 Clifton Rd., MS E-86, Atlanta, GA 30333
(800) 232-4636
e-mail: cdcinfo@cdc.gov
Web site: www.cdc.gov/ ncbddd

The CDC is a component of the U.S. Department of Health and Human Services and is the nation's premier health promotion, prevention, and preparedness agency. The NCBDDD is dedicated to helping people with birth defects and disabilities live life to the fullest. The CDC and the NCBDDD monitor birth defects prevalence, work to prevent birth defects, conduct birth defect research, and fund the birth defects research of others. The CDC and the NCBDDD publish numerous brochures, booklets, and fact sheets on specific birth defects, birth defects statistics, and birth defects prevention.

Cerebral Palsy International Research Foundation (CPIRF)
1025 Connecticut Ave. NW, Ste. 701
Washington, DC 20036
(202) 496-5060
e-mail: nmaher@cpirf .org
Web site: www.cpirf.org

CPIRF is a nonprofit organization dedicated to funding research and educational activities directly relevant to discovering the cause, cure, and evidence-based care for those with cerebral palsy and related developmental disabilities. CPIRF was formerly known as the United Cerebral Palsy Research and Educational Foundation, Inc. CPIRF provides grants for research and training on causes and prevention of cerebral palsy and on improving the quality of life of persons with cerebral palsy. The organization provides several fact sheets and videos on cerebral palsy, such as *Injury to the Preterm Brain* and *Cerebral Palsy, Part 1: Clinical Aspects of Injury to the Preterm Brain.*

Children's Hemiplegia and Stroke Association (CHASA)
4101 W. Green Oaks Blvd., Ste. 305, PMB 149, Arlington, TX 76016
(817) 492-4325
e-mail: info437@ chasa.org
Web site: www.chasa .org

CHASA is a nonprofit organization dedicated to improving the lives of children and families affected by pediatric stroke, cerebral palsy, and other causes of hemiplegia. CHASA serves families in a variety of locations in the United States as well as in other countries, through local meetings, online discussion groups, and educational Web sites. The organization's Web site offers research news, fact sheets, and brochures.

Children's Neurobiological Solutions (CNS) Foundation
909 E. First St., #12, Long Beach, CA 90802
(562) 331-0642
(866) 267-5580
e-mail: info@cns foundation.org
Web site: www.cns foundation.org

The CNS Foundation is a national nonprofit organization dedicated to improving the lives of children with neurological disorders by promoting research on brain repair and regeneration. The organization's primary goal is to promote the development of effective treatments for children with neurological disorders as quickly as possible. Toward this end, the foundation funds research and sponsors meetings about brain repair and regeneration, encourages young scientists to pursue children's neurological research, advocates for increased funding for children's neurological research, and educates families about options for treating their children. The organization has an electronic newsletter, *CNS eNews*.

March of Dimes Birth Defects Foundation
1275 Mamaroneck Ave., White Plains, NY 10605
(914) 428-7100
fax: (914) 428-8203
Web site: www.march ofdimes.com

The March of Dimes is one of the oldest U.S. organizations devoted to improving the health of babies. It raises money to help prevent birth defects, genetic disorders, premature births, and infant deaths. The March of Dimes carries out its mission through research, community service, education, and advocacy. The organization publishes a monthly e-mail newsletter called *Miracles*.

National Institute of Neurological Disorders and Stroke (NINDS)
PO Box 5801,
Bethesda, MD 20824
(301) 496-5751
(800) 352-9424
Web site: www.ninds
.nih.gov

NINDS is one of the twenty-seven institutes and centers that compose the National Institutes of Health. The mission of NINDS is to reduce the burden of neurological diseases borne by people all over the world. To accomplish this goal, it supports and conducts research, both basic and clinical, on the normal and diseased nervous system; fosters the training of investigators in the basic and clinical neurosciences; and seeks better understanding, diagnosis, treatment, and prevention of neurological disorders. The institute's Web site provides news articles and updates from workgroups and seminars on the latest brain research.

Pathways Awareness
150 N. Michigan Ave.
Ste. 2100, Chicago, IL
60601
(800) 955-2445
fax: (312) 893-6621
e-mail: friends@path
waysawareness.org
Web site: www.path
waysawareness.org

Pathways Awareness is a national nonprofit organization dedicated to increasing knowledge about the benefit of early detection and early therapy for infants and children with early motor developmental delays from neuromuscular conditions such as cerebral palsy. The organization supports parents by providing knowledge, information, and a sense of community as they guide their children on life's journey. Pathways Awareness provides informational materials such as DVDs, CDs, and brochures about babies' developmental milestones.

United Cerebral Palsy (UCP)
1660 L St. NW, Ste.
700, Washington, DC
20036
(202) 776-0406
(800) 872-5827
fax: (202) 776-0414
e-mail: national@ucp
.org
Web site: www.ucp.org

UCP is a national organization dedicated to serving and advocating for the more than 54 million Americans with disabilities. The organization works to advance the independence, productivity, and full citizenship of people with cerebral palsy and other disabilities through commitment to the principles of independence, inclusion, and self-determination. The UCP publishes the newsletters *Life Without Limits,* the *Capitol Insider,* and *UCPeople.*

FOR FURTHER READING

Books

Robert M. Baird, Stuart E. Rosenbaum, and S. Kay Toombs, eds., *Disability: The Social, Political, and Ethical Debate*. Amherst, NY: Prometheus Books, 2009.

Judy O. Berry, *Lifespan Perspectives on the Family and Disability*. Austin, TX: Pro-ed, 2009.

Ruth Bjorklund, *Cerebral Palsy*. New York: Benchmark Books, 2006.

Lúcia Willadino Braga and Aloysio Campos da Paz Jr., *The Child with Traumatic Brain Injury or Cerebral Palsy: A Context-Sensitive, Family-Based Approach to Development*. New York: Taylor & Francis, 2006.

Adriano Ferrari and Giovanni Cioni, *The Spastic Forms of Cerebral Palsy: A Guide to the Assessment of Adaptive Functions*. London: Springer, 2009.

Susan Gray, *Living with Cerebral Palsy*. Chanhassen, MN: Child's World, 2003.

Archie Hinchcliffe, *Children with Cerebral Palsy: A Manual for Therapists, Parents and Community Workers*. Thousand Oaks, CA: Sage, 2007.

Helen Horstmann and Eugene Bleck, *Orthopaedic Management in Cerebral Palsy*. London: Mac Keith, 2007.

Suzanne Kamata, *Love You to Pieces*. Boston: Beacon, 2008.

Marie Kennedy, *My Perfect Son Has Cerebral Palsy*. Bloomington, IN: 1stBooks, 2001.

Kay Harris Kriegsman, Elinor Zaslow, and Jennifer D'Zmura-Rechsteiner, *Taking Charge: Teenagers Talk About Life and Physical Disabilities*. Bethesda, MD: Woodbine House, 1992.

Sophie Levitt, *Treatment of Cerebral Palsy and Motor Delay*. Malden, MA: Blackwell, 2010.

Don Meyer, ed., *Thicker than Water: Essays by Adult Siblings of People with Disabilities*. Bethesda, MD: Woodbine House, 2009.

Freeman Miller and Steven Bachrach, *Cerebral Palsy: A Complete Guide for Caregiving*. Baltimore: Johns Hopkins University Press, 2006.

Shelley Nixon, *From Where I Sit: Making My Way with Cerebral Palsy*. New York: Scholastic, 1999.

Christos Panteliadis and Hans-Michael Strassburg, *Cerebral Palsy: Principles and Management*. New York: George Thieme, 2004.

Philip R. Reilly, *Is It in Your Genes? The Influence of Genes on Common Disorders and Diseases That Affect You and Your Family*. New York: Cold Spring Harbor Laboratory Press, 2004.

Periodicals

Heidi Anttila et al. "Effectiveness of Physical Therapy Interventions for Children with Cerebral Palsy: A Systematic Review," *BMC Pediatrics*, April 24, 2008.

Stacy Beck et al. "The Worldwide Incidence of Preterm Birth," *Bulletin of the World Health Organization*, January 2010.

Abraham B. Bergman, "The Right of Children with Disabilities to Have Fun," *Archives of Pediatrics & Adolescent Medicine*, November 2007.

Peter Burton, Lynn Lethbridge, and Shelley Phipps, "Children with Disabilities and Chronic Conditions and Longer Term Parental Health," *Journal of Socio-Economics Detail*, June 2008.

Leon Chaitow et al. "Modifying the Effects of Cerebral Palsy: The Gregg Mozgala Story," *Journal of Bodywork & Movement Therapies*, April 2010.

Gareth Cook, "Chinese Surgeon's Claims About Cell Implants Disputed," *Boston Globe*, June 19, 2006.

E. Davis et al. "The Impact of Caring for a Child with Cerebral Palsy: Quality of Life for Mothers and Fathers," *Child: Care, Health and Development*, January 2010.

Bernard Dickens and Rebecca Cook, "The Legal Effects of Fetal Monitoring Guidelines," *International Journal of Gynecology and Obstetrics*, February 2010.

Batya Engel-Yeger, Tal Jarus, Dana Anaby, and Mary Law, "Differences in Patterns of Participation Between Youths with Cerebral Palsy and Typically Developing Peers," *American Journal of Occupational Therapy*, January/February 2009.

Lisa Girion, "Death, Drug Reactions Spur Concern About Botox Safety," *Los Angeles Times*, February 9, 2008.

Michelle E. Kelly, David Legg, Joe Bentle, and Wilson Sierman Burnett, "Wrestling and Children with Cerebral Palsy, *Palaestra*, Winter 2009.

Michael D. Kogan, Bonnie B. Strickland, and Paul W. Newacheck, "Building Systems of Care: Findings from the National Survey of Children with Special Health Care Needs," *Pediatrics*, December 2009.

L.A. Koman et al. "Cerebral Palsy," *Lancet*, vol. 363, 2004.

Gregory Liptak, "Health and Well Being of Adults with Cerebral Palsy," *Current Opinion in Neurology*, April 21, 2008.

Anna Martin, Patricia A. Burtner, Janet Poole, and John Phillips, "Case Report: ICF-Level Changes in a Preschooler After Constraint-Induced Movement Therapy," *American Journal of Occupational Therapy*, May/June 2008.

Victoria Page, "The Power of Words (and Finally . . .)," *Paraplegia News*, March 2009.

Robert J. Palisano et al. "Social and Community Participation of Children and Youth with Cerebral Palsy Is Associated with Age and Gross Motor Function," *Physical Therapy Detail*, December 2009.

Peter Rosenbaum, "Cerebral Palsy: What Parents and Doctors Want to Know," *British Medical Journal*, May 3, 2003.

Martin Staudt, "Brain Plasticity Following Early Life Brain Injury: Insights from Neuroimaging," *Seminars in Perinatology*, February 2010.

E. Taub et al. "Efficacy of Constraint-Induced Movement Therapy for Children with Cerebral Palsy with Asymmetric Motor Impairment," *Pediatrics*, February 2004.

Michael Wilkes and Margaret Johns, "Informed Consent and Shared Decision-Making: A Requirement to Disclose to Patients Off-Label Prescriptions," *PloS Medicine*, November 2008.

Rosa Zarrinkalam et al. "CP or Not CP? A Review of Diagnoses in a Cerebral Palsy Register," *Pediatric Neurology*, March 2010.

Internet Sources

Ginni Buller, "First-Time Mom with Spastic Cerebral Palsy," National Center on Physical Activity and Disability, November 10, 2008. www.ncpad.org/yourwrites/fact_sheet.php?sheet=480.

Mayo Clinic, "Cerebral Palsy." www.mayoclinic.com/health/cerebralpalsy/DS00302.

Medline Plus, "Cerebral Palsy." www.nlm.nih.gov/medlineplus/cerebralpalsy.html#cat28.

ScienceDaily, "10,000 People in World-First Cerebral Palsy Study," July 2, 2008. www.sciencedaily.com/releases/2008/07/080702160952.htm.

INDEX